LIFE IS A FATAL DISEASE

To
Betsy with
affection and friendship

MHO —

LIFE IS A FATAL DISEASE

DISEASE

✦

(Reflections on a Lifetime)

Enzo Krahl, M.D.

iUniverse, Inc.
New York Lincoln Shanghai

LIFE IS A FATAL DISEASE
(Reflections on a Lifetime)

iUniverse books may be ordered through booksellers or by contacting:

iUniverse
2021 Pine Lake Road, Suite 100
Lincoln, NE 68512
www.iuniverse.com
1-800-Authors (1-800-288-4677)

ISBN-13: 978-0-595-35970-7 (pbk)
ISBN-13: 978-0-595-80421-4 (ebk)
ISBN-10: 0-595-35970-1 (pbk)
ISBN-10: 0-595-80421-7 (ebk)

Printed in the United States of America

To the memory of my Grandmother Regina Aub, who believed in the Goodness of Man, and the Power and Justice of God, and who lost Her Life in the gas chambers of the Risiera San Sabba in Trieste.

Contents

INTRODUCTION

Many books have been published recently on subjects such as sex, diet, financial success, leisure time, physical fitness, and living with a cancer patient. Each subject has been dealt with as a separate entity without uniting all these aspects and addressing the total issue, which is LIFE.

I decided to write this book many years ago while I was still engaged in a very busy surgical practice. I was taking care of a patient in his mid fifties who had had surgery for a carcinoma of the bowel one year earlier, and was again in the hospital because of metastatic disease. The cancer had spread to the abdominal cavity and to the lungs, and it was causing pain because of recurring episodes of small bowel obstruction. That particular morning, while I was making rounds, he looked at me with an expression that revealed a mixture of anguish and terror, and while he was holding on to my hand he said: "Doctor, am I going to die?" I was not prepared for that question and it took me a few seconds before I answered: "Yes you are Walter, of course you are going to die, and so am I, but I don't know when. You see, Walter, we all are going to die, because Life is a fatal disease".

Walter was an average middle class head of a family. He had been working as a self-employed insurance agent and had achieved a level of sufficient financial security to start enjoying the fruits of his labor. As happens so often in life, he was struck by severe major illness when he least expected it He was frightened by the nature of his illness, and by the thought that death was watching over him.
"Doctor" he said, "who gives you the right to talk like this? I don't know who gives me the right to talk like this, but I know what gives me this right, and that is the fact that we all are in the same boat, and that when I talk to you I am addressing myself as well".

We all know that while we are going through life, eventually this will come to an end, but the thought had not struck me in its true terms until I happened to make this remark to this dying man. It seemed to comfort him. This thought stayed with me and grew in my mind. It has given me a more meaningful and appreciative outlook on life itself. Of course we all know that we are not alive on this earth forever, but we don't really think about it. We take our being here and being well for granted, and only when we get old and when we get sick do we give this matter some casual thought.

Centuries ago the Romans said: "Memento mori". They did not say it in a morbid depressive sense, but in a very sobering and realistic and essentially humbling way. "Memento mori, remember you shall die". One should be able to grasp this concept for what it really means, before one might build on it. One has to accept this view with serenity before one can expand on it objectively. I asked an old man one day to what he attributed his serenity, and he answered without hesitation" my friend, serenity is the art to accept the inevitable".

We can look more objectively to ourselves and to our relationships with other human beings and with society if we can accept this premise without anxiety. I will analyze these relationships with the logic learned from this assumption.

Many seemingly complex situations and complex relationships can be reduced to simple equations when they are seen through the glasses of this simple truth: "Life is a fatal disease". "Memento mori". Joy to live, humility to die.

This is the spirit with which I am writing this book. It expresses the experience of a lifetime of observations of human beings and events, and the lessons learned from them. I am grateful for having lived, and for the feelings and experiences that made me alive while living. Life should be a vibrant experience. The most important thing in life is appreciation of happiness. This is why these notes, though objectively stating that Life is a fatal disease, should be looked at as an Ode to Life.

I

I have dedicated this book to the memory of my maternal grandmother. She was born in 1870, and she spent a great deal of time with my sister and me when we were children and young teenagers. The stories she told us about her life, her values, and the society in which she grew up, plus my personal experiences during my lifetime, allowed me to have an overview of life in the Western world from the late 19th century to the 21st century. I shall reflect on these events and experiences of my life, from a protected childhood to humiliation and persecution, and eventually to survival and rehabilitation.

I was born in Fiume on April 22nd, 1924, 18 months after Mussolini's fascist regime had been installed in Rome by King Victor Emanuel III, and 37 days after Fiume had been annexed to Italy. The population of the city was of various ethnic backgrounds, Austro-Hungarian, Croat, and Italian, while the surrounding countryside was mainly inhabited by Croat peasants. The majority of the people were Catholic: there were however some Greek Orthodox, Jews, and very few Protestants. The name Fiume means "river" in Italian, and the city is located at the mouth of the river Eneo, in the northeast corner of the Adriatic Sea. Originally it was a Roman town called Tarsatica, and was inhabited by fishermen. There is to this day a Roman arch standing in the "old city".

In the year 998 the Greek emperor Basil II granted the Republic of Venice the protectorate of the Dalmatian coast. In the 18th century, during the reign of Maria Teresa, Fiume became part of the Austrian empire, and in the 19th century Fiume became a Hungarian port under the dual Austro-Hungarian monarchy.

Toward the end of World War I, in September and October 1918, some citizens attempted to place Fiume under Croat control, but the majority of the population was against it, and on October 30th there was a referendum, and five men, called the "Argonauts" were sent by motorboat to Venice to call on the Allied troops, especially the Italian troops, to come and occupy the city. On November 4th, 1918 two Italian navy ships, the Stocco and the San Marco, entered the harbor, and the commander of this fleet took charge of the city without a shot being fired. The Croats settled in Susak, east of the river Eneo.

On November 17th, 1918 Italian troops followed by American, British, and French troops under the allied command of General Grazioli entered the city, and the General assumed the power of Governor of Fiume. On February 12, 1919 Mussolini, still an unknown politician, came to Fiume and gave a speech encouraging the unification to Italy. He was booed, and left town. On September 12th, 1919 the poet Gabriele D'Annunzio arrived with about 300 Legionnaires, and took over the city. The Allied troops, including the Italian troops, left the city without a fight, and withdrew a few kilometers west to the resort town of Abbazia. The Legionnaires behaved like gangsters, requisitioning and stealing. Little by little they grew to about 10.000. D'Annunzio formed a provisional Government of the Carnaro and eventually the Regency of the Carnaro. Not one person from Fiume was part of this Government. Captain Vidala' was chief of police, and Mr. Giuriati Minister of the Interior. They printed their own currency and stamps. D'Annunzio's tyranny continued. Some of his officers (Captain Cocco and Raffaele Cantoni) opposed his megalomania, were tried and convicted by a court of Legionnaires, and fled to safety to Italy.

On November 12th, 1920 the treaty of Rapallo stipulated that Italy would obtain Istria that Yugoslavia would obtain Dalmatia, and that Fiume would become an independent free city.

On December 24th, 1920 the Italian battleship Andrea Doria entered the port of Fiume and gave D'Annunzio an ultimatum of 6 hours to surrender and to abandon the city. D'Annunzio refused the ultimatum, and the ship opened fire while the Italian troops from Abbazia entered the city. In the city itself, the population revolted against the Legionnaires, and a bloody battle followed with many victims. The destroyer Esperia was blown up in the harbor with the loss of the entire crew. This day became known as "Il Natale di sangue", the bloody Christmas. On December 26th, 1920 the Italian troops occupied the city and took D'Annunzio and most of the Legionnaires back to Italy as prisoners. Mussolini rehabilitated D'Annunzio and confined him to a splendid "house arrest" in a large villa on Lago di Garda. There he spent the rest of his life giving speeches from the bow of a ship grounded in front of his mansion. He died there in 1938.

In January 1921 Riccardo Zanella was elected President of the independent free city of Fiume. Zanella had been congressman from Fiume to the Austro-Hungarian Parliament. He formed a regular Government with citizens from Fiume, and life returned to normal.

On March 3rd, 1922, in a coup d'etat, Italian troops entered the city under the command of General Grazioli, and Zanella and his cabinet were indicted for treason. Being able to leave town, they found refuge first in England, and later in the United States. The civil powers were taken over by a Commissioner, Mr. Costelli. On February 6th, 1924 Victor Emanuel III, King of Italy came to visit Fiume. Later that month there was a referendum about annexation to Italy, or maintenance of the independent free status. Somehow the ballots were burned, but it was declared that the majority had voted for annexation. Annexation to Italy occurred on March 16th, 1924.

When I was born, there was my sister Alessandrina (Drina) at home, two years older than I. My parents had an Austrian governess for us, so that I learned Italian and German as a child, and could speak both languages equally well. When I was five years old, my parents replaced the Austrian governess with a French-speaking governess, and Drina and I learned French.

There were two public parks in Fiume, and every afternoon, Monday through Friday, my sister and I would go to one of the parks to play. Our Grandmother, affectionately called Nonna, would come to our home every afternoon around three o'clock and bring a praline to each of us. It was an expected ritual. We would leave the house soon thereafter and walk with her and the governess to one of the parks, and return around six thirty. At the park we would play with some of our friends, and listen to what Nonna had to say. Some of our friends were children of our parents' friends, and some were children whose families were not known to us. Some of the children came with their governesses, and others came alone. We played with all of them. There was no social distinction, and all the children behaved well, and listened to the suggestions and the instructions of the adults. Most of them were Catholic, some were Jewish; only one family was Protestant. Religion was never an issue, until the fateful racial laws of 1938.

Walking to and from the park with my sister, the governess and Nonna, I would talk and listen to her, and I came to learn her philosophy of life. She used to say: "When you play with fire, you may get burned ". This was supposed to teach us two things: first not to put ourselves at risk, and second, that if you put yourself at risk, you can not blame anybody else for your action, and that you have to take full responsibility for being in that predicament in the first place. Nowadays people like to blame other people for their problems, and like to point fingers at tobacco makers and MacDonald's for example. What they should do is point a finger at themselves or a mirror.

She would always encourage Drina and me to rely on our own resources and to do the best we could with what we had. She used to say: "Bad luck does not come from God", and "The closest helping hand is at the end of your own arm". She would point out that usually children follow the examples set by their parents and their environment, and that "the apple does not fall far from the tree". She would say that it was important to be frugal and save in good times, because in bad times there was nothing to save, and that "one could always find a gold nail near a gold carriage". "Do not be afraid" she used to say, "God will protect you if you are a good person". This did not prove to be true in her case, as she lost her life in a gas chamber. I have ever since felt that if ever there was a God, He or She certainly died in Auschwitz.

As we got older, Nonna would not see us every day, and would not bring us pralines any longer, but she would still be very much part of our lives, and share with us her philosophy of life. "It takes a lifetime to prove that one is honest" She used to say, "but it takes only one instance to prove that one is a liar or a crook."

Nonna's basic rule of life was: "Do not do unto others what you don't want others to do unto you". Another favorite saying of hers was one that to this day has formed the foundation of my social attitude: "Wer das Kleine nicht ehrt, is das Grosse nicht wert". (He, who does not appreciate the little things, is not worthy of big rewards).

As I mentioned in the history of Fiume, the city was annexed to Italy in March 1924. The Fascist Party took over the Government of Italy in October 1922, so that the population of Fiume never experienced an Italian government that was not headed by Mussolini. Italy and Fascism became synonymous, and belonging to the Fascist Party became a matter of fact without any particular significance for Christians and Jews alike. My father never joined the Fascist Party, but he was president of a privately owned bank, and he did not need it for his employment. He had also been a Mason, and Masonry was outlawed under the Fascist regime. He was a well-known person in town, and was asked several times to join the Party, but he refused. He was also asked to change his name to an Italian sounding Carli, but he refused, saying that only people who owe money that they can not repay change their names, and that he did not have any debts.

I joined the Fascist youth organization (Balilla) when I started first grade in public school, as did every other student; it was compulsory. In the public elementary schools (they were the only schools in town) Catholicism was taught two hours a week, and the class was graded like any other subject. Non-Catholic students were excused from class, and received their religious instruction in Sunday school. In February 1929 Mussolini had signed a concordat with Pope Pius XI in which the Pope recognized Italy's jurisdiction over Rome, and Italy recognized the clergy as having jurisdiction over marriage and the family. Divorce was not legal. Italy also guaranteed financial support of all Churches regardless of denomination.

During my childhood Fiume had a population of about 55,000 of which about 2200 were Jews, a fairly large percentage. Most of the Jews were of central European ancestry, and belonged to the middle class (professional people and merchants). Most of the blue-collar population was of Slavic descent. Everybody got along well with each other, and respected each other. The surroundings reflected the customs and the way of life of "Middle Europe" embodied by the culture and traditions of the multiethnic Austro-Hungarian Empire in the post Napoleonic era. The middle class had emerged, and the aristocracy had lost most of its political and economic power, and transferred to the public at large that tradition of culture and urbanity. In one word we lived in a "civilized" society.

I firmly believe that the framers of the Treaty of Versailles after World War I made a crucial and eventually tragic mistake: instead of breaking up the Austro-Hungarian Empire, they should have broken up the German Reich. Had they done so, World War Two would probably have been avoided.

While my Father was alive, we used to spend part of the summer in the Villa Irenea in Abbazia. Abbazia had been until 1900 the playground of the aristocracy. After the turn of the 20th century the middle class had taken over that playground. Many years later, in the early 1960's, I took my American wife Anne to Fiume and Abbazia (at this time, Rijeka and Opatjia in Tito's Yugoslavia). I had not been back for over 25 years. We went to have lunch at Pepi's small restaurant, in the harbor, noted for its scampi risotto. The owner remembered me as a child. The place was filled with Croatian blue-collar workers. After lunch I told Anne, "I can understand now how the aristocrats felt when the middle class took over their turf."

II

In 1934, I was 10 years old, my Father was 51, and he had not felt well for several weeks. At about that time Dr. Whipple had devised an operation at Presbyterian Hospital in New York City for resection of the pancreas. My Father was diagnosed to have cancer of the pancreas and he decided to go to Budapest to have the surgery because Professor Adam of the University of Budapest was one of the few surgeons in Europe who was doing the Whipple procedure. The operation went well, but unfortunately on the fifth postoperative day my Father suffered an uncontrollable internal hemorrhage and died.

My Mother brought the body back to Fiume to be buried. At the time of his death my Father was President of the Hebrew Congregation in Fiume. He was not an observant Jew; we did not keep kosher in our home, and he worked at the bank on Saturdays. For him being religious meant, "not to do unto others what you don't want others to do unto you". His two other favorite sayings were, "early to bed and early to rise make a man healthy, wealthy, and wise" and "it is better to be alone than in bad company."

I was 10 years old. Our lives changed, but we were still able to live comfortably. My mother received a pension from the bank, and we owned our home and some real estate. My father always felt that in order to be reasonably safe under most circumstances, one should divide one's assets into three equal parts: one currency stocks and bonds, two teal estate, and three gold and precious metals. My mother continued that custom.

At age ten, I could not understand why such a good man should die: how we could believe in "Divine Justice" when such things were allowed to happen. Probably there was no "plan" and that "things", good things and bad, occurred simply by accident. It followed that our life was here on Earth, and that afterlife was simply a myth. People who believed in afterlife in Heaven were very lucky because they were living with that hope, and would never find out that it was only a dream, since we know nothing after life on earth.

Human beings aspire to justice. The concept of an afterlife is based on this aspiration. God will reward or punish you. It is really always easy to promise something if you don't have to deliver it. It is much more difficult to provide social justice during this life on earth. Politicians and salesmen eventually have to fulfill their promises, or they will be discredited. In religion there is no such need: rewards are promised in "Heaven." No proof is necessary for such promises. It is a matter of "faith." Under these circumstances any promise can be made. This is what has made religions so popular and so powerful. It is easy to say, "God wants you to do this or not to do that, and He will reward you or punish you in Heaven." He who speaks in the name of God does not have to deliver anything, and the great majority of people through history have been "believers." It is a feeling that gives great comfort. For this reason "believers" are very lucky because they will never know that death on earth is the "end."

I believe that there is reward for a "good life," and that this reward is the satisfaction that one has behaved honestly and that one has done one's best to contribute to the well being of this earth and its inhabitants. It also occurred to me that "Religion" is a vehicle of human longings, and that "God" was created by man to serve as an image for all the perfections that Man dreams for himself. In worshipping "God," Man is really worshipping his own ideals.

Little by little the Middle Europe atmosphere was progressively replaced by the motto of Mussolini's Italy: "Credere, obbedire, combattere" (To believe, to obey, to fight)—There were banners with these words across the streets, and also: "Il Duce ha sempre ragione" (The Duce is always right). Nonna would say: "Nobody is always right, only bad people want to fight all the time; God created a beautiful peaceful world, and we should try and keep it that way". I was told not to discuss these signs and these issues either in school or with my friends. I was also told not to believe one word of what those banners said, because it was utter nonsense.

Even if officially the constitution was not abolished in Italy when Mussolini took office, and even if the Crown was not deprived of its prerogatives, there is no doubt that the policies of the Fascist Government in Italy could not have been carried out without the complicity of the King. It can be added that many western democracies supported for many years, politically and economically, the fascist regime because they feared the potential spread of socialism.

As I mentioned earlier, I had difficulty developing blind faith. I was fascinated by the wonders of nature, the beauty and diversity of the Adriatic Sea and the mountains of the Carso, the fierceness of the storms and the variety of animals and plants. The willful planning of all this by a Supreme Power seemed unlikely to me. I was more attracted to the reality of chance and fate with earthly consequences, rather that divine planning with celestial rewards and infernal punishments. All the years since my childhood and all my life experiences have only reinforced this belief. Life is a fatal disease: one is born here on earth, and it is up to each individual to live his or her life to the best of one's ability.

Many years later, one morning at breakfast, my daughter Katie, age nine, asked me: "Dad, why are we here?" I certainly was not prepared for such a question, but I came up with this answer: "To leave the world a better place than we found it when we were born". She seemed satisfied with this answer, and I was proud of it".

III

On January 30th, 1933, Adolph Hitler was appointed Chancellor of Germany. On March 5th of the same year, elections were held in Germany and Hitler's Nazi party won a majority of the seats in the Bundestag. Everybody in Italy knew at the time that the Nazis and Hitler did not like the Jews, but nobody, to my knowledge, suspected that what eventually occurred would happen. Not even after the promulgation of the Nurenberg laws of September 15th, 1935. My father's brothers and sisters were living at that time in Central Europe (Hungary and Romania), and they did not seem particularly concerned about the happenings in Germany.

Mussolini was absorbed by the bold dream of an empire, and on October 2nd, 1935, invaded Ethiopia. Italy at that time had three colonies: Eritrea and Somalia in East Africa since the late 1890's and Libya in North Africa after Turkey's defeat in 1911. In order to ship troops and material to East Africa for the war with Ethiopia, the Italian navy had to cross the Suez Canal controlled at that time by Great Britain. The shipment of arms and soldiers was allowed only upon payment of specific duties per weapon and per man in gold. Mussolini ordered each Italian married woman to contribute her wedding band to pay these duties. My father had just died, and my mother was not about to part with her wedding band. She bought one at a jewelry store, and complied with the law by donating the new ring. I am quite sure that other women did the same thing. These rings however did not suffice to pay for the war, and Hitler's Germany offered financial help to Mussolini. On May 9th, 1936 Italy annexed Ethiopia, and on November 1st of the same year Mussolini proclaimed the Berlin-Rome axis. Foreign secretary Anthony Eden apparently had not learned any thing from Machiavelli, who in the 15th century had advised, "never to irritate enemies, but to either caress them or kill them"!

It was not a coincidence that on July 25th 1934 when the Nazis murdered the Austrian Chancellor Engelbert Dollfuss, and the German troops were about to enter Austria, Mussolini sent two Italian divisions to the Brenner Pass stopping Hitler from invading Austria, and that on March 12th, 1938, Mussolini did not move one finger, allowing German troops to enter Austria unmolested and allowing Hitler to annex Austria.

My friends and I were young teenagers at that time, and we did not pay much attention to what was happening around us. It seemed almost as remote as the war that was taking place in Asia between Japan and China, or the civil war in Spain, where Italian troops were actively supporting General Franco. It meant nothing to us that Germany had resigned from the League of Nations on October 14, 1933, and that Italy had withdrawn from the League of Nations on December 11, 1937. It did not seem either interesting or important to us that while Italy and Germany were governed by reactionary dictatorships, Great Britain and France were experimenting with Labor and Socialist Governments respectively. It was a time when I was more interested in humanities than current events and politics.

All this changed abruptly and drastically when on October 6, 1938, the Italian Government issued the racial laws. Before that time Jews were rarely discussed in Italy, and then only to say that Italy did not have a Jewish problem. Jews had lived in Rome since before the first century B.C. One of Mussolini's very close friends was the Jewish Italian writer Margherita Sarfatti.

In 1932 the well-known Jewish German writer Emil Ludwig published a series of interviews with Mussolini, which became an authorized biography, and were translated by the Italian Government into twelve languages. The title was "Talks with Mussolini." In this book Mussolini stated that purity of race can not be proven biologically, that there was no anti-Semitism in Italy, that there was no Jewish problem in Italy because the Jews had always been good citizens and good soldiers, and that they occupied honorably many responsible positions in the Italian society and Army.

Luigi Barzini, in his book "The Italians," describes with some detail the character of Mussolini and the effect of his government on Italy and the Italians. He fails to mention the racial laws of 1938. Thousands of lives of active and devoted Italian citizens were affected, many of them ruined, but Barzini does not think that this nefarious act is worth mentioning. Instead it seems to me that it defines somehow Mussolini's cowardice, and his willingness to do anything to promote his importance in the eyes of Hitler. Since Mussolini assumed that Hitler would control the European continent Mussolini wanted to be a full partner. It did not matter whom he hurt or destroyed, it was only he who mattered. This is the man who ordered the killing of Matteotti, of the Rosselli brothers, and of his own son in law, Galeazzo Ciano. History should remember him for what he was: a pompous, unscrupulous, self centered, ambitious, ineffective coward.

In spite of all this, he was a gifted orator. Trau is one of the many cities on the Dalmatian coast that was founded by the Republic of Venice. The emblem of the Venetian Republic was the lion. In the early 1930's, an unruly Yugoslav mob destroyed a Venetian stone lion in the harbor of Trau. The lion had been there for centuries. Mussolini made a short statement: "Solo un popolo incivile e barbaro crede che scolpendo la pietra si cancelli la storia". (Only an uncivilized and barbarian people believe that by pounding a stone one can erase history).

Anti-Semitism had been practiced through the centuries on a religious ground. Jews had been persecuted as "Christ killers" and as people who would use blood of Christian children to prepare matzo and other ritual food. Baptism however would redeem the sinners and bring about salvation of their soul. In many countries at different times the Catholic Church would force Jews to either convert, be expelled from the country, or be burned as "heretics". Martin Luther and his followers were not much kinder to the Jews. The persecutors never mentioned that Jesus, Peter, Paul, and the other apostles were all Jews.

During the late 18th century, and in the 19th and 20th centuries, and because of the enlightenment and of the loss of some of the power of the Church, anti-Semitism switched from a religious motive to a "race" concept. Could the Jews, who were living in separate groups within a nation, be part of the "Nation?" Could the Jews who were mainly involved in trade and finance be considered part of the general population mainly involved in agriculture and labor? It is interesting that this should have been pointed out, among others, by a converted Jew, Karl Marx. Africans and Orientals could be easily identified among Caucasians, and could be easily discriminated against, but Jews were Caucasians and had lived in the same countries for centuries. For the purpose of isolating the Jews from other Caucasians, the "Aryan" concept was introduced and the "religious" anti-Semitism became a "racial" anti-Semitism. Conversion to Christianity did not help anymore. It is ironic, however, that the social life and the basic Laws of "Western Civilization" were based on "honor your father and your mother, do not steal, do not commit adultery, do not commit murder, do not covet your neighbor's wife, cow or ass, do not bear false witness, sanctify the Sabbath and take a day of rest for yourself, your servants and your animals" which were written thousands of years earlier by wise Jewish men who proclaimed the above as "God given Commandments."

IV

The racial laws did not cause any monetary hardship to my family since my mother was not working, and therefore could not lose a job, but my sister and I were not allowed to go to classes in the public schools. The law allowed Jewish students to take an examination at the end of the school year, and if they passed the examination, they were promoted to the next grade, but they could not attend classes. This policy was in effect for grade school, middle school and high school, but Jews were not allowed to enroll in any university, nor were they allowed to take exams there. For the first time, and out of the blue sky, I found myself to be "different." Not being in school, I could not participate in after school activities with my friends, and I would automatically lose contact with them. I was also expelled from the city tennis club, where I had played successfully for a number of years, and where that same year 1938 I was junior champion.

That same year I started to write a diary, which I kept writing for many years. In the diary I wrote that every individual seems to have three different personalities: the way other people see him, the way he sees himself, and the way he really is. The relationship with most of my former schoolmates eventually became non existent, and I became closer to other Jewish students and to a couple of slightly older Catholic teenagers with whom I shared love for classical music and opera. We were still allowed to go to the theater. My sister and I took private lessons from Jewish teachers who had lost their jobs, and from teachers who were teaching in the public schools that we could not attend. Sometimes these same teachers would grade us with exams at the end of the year.

All these circumstances, I believe, contributed to my growing up faster than my contemporaries, and made me look at society from the outside trying to understand why the law established that I was "different". I decided at that time that I wanted to become a surgeon; I wanted not only to survive, but also to prove that I could be as good as anybody. It also occurred to me that in the doctor's office even a king has to take off his pants.

In spite of all the evidence to the contrary, we did not believe that the racial laws would persist. We did not believe that the people in Italy and in Germany would tolerate such discrimination and persecution, and that countries who had produced Dante and Verdi, Michelangelo and the Renaissance, Goethe, Schiller and Beethoven could sink to such a level of barbarism. Unfortunately we underestimated the might of dictatorships. Most people behaved in a matter of fact way. Social contacts continued for the most part, but there was no outrage against the injustices. Most non-Jewish friends and citizens in general said that the law was unfair, but that it was the law. My grandmother put it at a different level. She trusted in God: He was just and powerful, and He would never allow these injustices to continue.

There was only one group in town that was quite vocal about this issue. It was the GUF (Gruppo Universitario Fascista), group of Fascist University students, who had a meeting hall on the second floor of a building on the Corso, the pedestrian main street downtown, used as a shopping area and where people would walk up and down in the evening to meet friends and to spend some time at the end of the working day, before dinner time. The GUF had a loudspeaker and would announce the accomplishments of the Fascist regime and play some music. Their favorite song was one they made up themselves: "Zifut con le treciette le valigiette tii faraa" saying in local dialect that a Jew with small braids shall pack his small suitcase and leave.

The beating of Jews, the burning and the plundering of their properties and the desecration of synagogues that occurred in Germany and Austria, did not occur in Italy. The racial laws were followed, but quite reluctantly in many instances. Why did the Jews put up with this, and not leave the countries in which they were "legally" persecuted? The main reason was that they felt they were "citizens" of that country, and that they thought that these unjust laws would not last much longer. The other reason was that after World War I, it had become necessary to have a passport and a visa to move from one country to another. In 1492, when Catholic Spain expelled the Jews, many of them found refuge in other European Catholic countries, and in the 1550's, during the reign of Mary Tudor, thousands of English Protestants found refuge in Holland, After the edict of Nantes was revoked in 1685, a very large number of French Huguenots fled France to find refuge in Switzerland, England, Holland, and other Protestant countries. Until World War I, individuals who had not committed a crime could move freely from country to country, and did not need identification cards, passports, visas or work permits. All this changed after the war, and all these documents became necessary. Some countries, the United States among them, established immigration quotas for different countries, and no country seemed particularly interested in admitting large numbers of Jews. The tragic fate of the passengers of the boat "Saint Louis" in May-June 1939 is good evidence to support this statement. The Jewish German passengers of this ship had permission to enter the United States but had to wait for the valid date of the "German quota." They were hoping to be allowed to stay in Cuba until the U.S. visas would become effective. Their Cuban visas, however, were declared invalid by Cuba's president Frederico Laredo Bru, and the "Saint Louis" was ordered to leave Cuba's waters. In spite of guarantees of support by the Jewish Joint Distribution Committee, neither Cuba nor the United States allowed the refugees to debark. They were taken back to France, Belgium and the Netherlands, and when Germany occupied these countries a few months later, they were arrested and sent to concentration camps where they perished.

Most people profess the belief in one God. The Jews were the first people to reject paganism and to establish monotheism: one God. Through the story of Moses and the burning bush on Mount Sinai, and the promulgation of the Ten Commandments, the Jews laid the foundation of moral behavior in the Western world. In spite of all this, Christians and Moslems have invoked the authority of the same God to persecute, plunder and kill the "infidel" Jew.

Mendelssohn, Heine, Disraeli, and Gustav Mahler, among many others, had to convert to Christianity in order to be accepted professionally and socially. This unfair attitude, most common toward Jews, is not exclusive to them. Many years later, I was playing golf one day with a very good friend of mine who pointed to a foursome ahead of us and said: "I went to school with those fellows, we were all kids together in Savannah. We were all Southern Baptists; I am still a Baptist, but now they are all Episcopalians: for social reasons, you understand!"

V

On September 1, 1939, Germany invaded Poland and annexed Danzig. Italy declared neutrality. On September 3, 1939, Great Britain and France declared war on Germany after Germany refused to stop the invasion of Poland, Australia and New Zealand joined Great Britain and also declared war on Germany. In Fiume most people, Christians and Jews alike, felt that this would finally eliminate Hitler and the Nazi regime. Only a few "professional Fascists" expressed support for Germany, and were disappointed that Italy stayed on the sidelines. Unfortunately the events proved that France was a paper tiger, and that Great Britain was a tenacious and determined, but unprepared lion.

There is no question in my mind that the two men primarily responsible for Hitler's defeat are Winston Churchill, who refused to surrender after the defeat of France, and Hirohito, who by bombing Pearl Harbor brought the determination and the might of the United States into the war. There is no question in my mind that the United States would not have entered the war had she not been attacked by Japan. In fact the United States declared war on Japan, and Germany declared war on the United States. We also owe a great deal of gratitude to the Serb leadership of the Yugoslav Army. By not surrendering after having been attacked by Italy and Germany, Serbia caused the attack on the Soviet Union to be delayed by one month, allowing "General Winter" to stop the German advance before the total collapse of the Soviet army.

I followed the war in the Italian press and on the radio, and every evening at seven o'clock I listened to the Italian broadcast on the BBC by Colonel Stevens. Listening to the BBC was strictly forbidden and punishable by prison or internment. A number of my friends did the same thing, and sometimes we would confide in each other on this subject. None of us ever betrayed the trust or the friendship. Some of my older non-Jewish friends were being drafted into the Italian army, and most of them were unhappy about it. The war was not popular.

My sister Drina was an outstanding student. When the racial laws came into effect in the fall of 1938, she had two years left to graduate from the "Liceo Classico". Her classmates and teachers continued to consider her "the best student." She studied privately and took examinations at the end of each year. She graduated in 1940. The Jewish congregation in Milano had established a private paro-chial University with only one major, chemistry. Jewish professors who had lost their jobs because of the same racial laws did the teaching. About 30 students enrolled, and Drina was among them. She rented a room in Milano, and lived there during the school year. She continued to be an outstanding student. She made new friends, and some of them visited us during the summer in Fiume or in the resort town of Abbazia. When she died in February 1944 she was only four months away from a PhD in chemistry.

In the spring of 1941, Italy invaded Yugoslavia. Fiume and the other border towns were evacuated. Our family and a number of our friends went to Firenze. Drina was in Milano. My mother and I and some cousins checked in at the Vil-lino Montebello. One of the cousins, who had lost his job in Fiume because of the racial laws, had been doing some business in Prato, a town near Firenze, and had been staying at the Villino Montebello, where he had befriended the owner Mr. Leoni. We found out that the Jewish congregation of Firenze had a parochial school, and I was welcomed to join the junior class of the Liceo. I made new friends, and for the first time since the racial laws I experienced again a classroom atmosphere. After a few weeks we moved to an apartment, and I finished the school year, returning however to Fiume for the year-end examinations.

I always had a love for opera. My parents had taken me to hear Rossini's "Bar-ber of Seville" when I was five years old, and since then I have not missed many performances that were given within a reachable distance. I attended a number of performances that year in Firenze, and among them "Andrea Chenier", one of my favorite operas. Gerard's words in his aria "Nemico della Patria" rang in my ears then, and are still ringing, "Fare del mondo un Pantheon, gli uomini in Dii mutare" (Make the world a Pantheon. turn men into Gods). The war, the trage-dies, the injustices, all the suffering so unnecessary and so unfair, while a little good will could make life so much more pleasant for everybody. The same words and wish apply today in this unstable world. More than half a century later, I would by chance notice on the hilltop town of Castell'Arquato a monument in a small park behind the Visconti Castle and the inscription caught my eye: "vicino a te s'acquieta l'irrequieta anima mia" (near you my restless soul finds peace) which are the words from the love duet of the finale of Andrea Chenier. I found out that Castell'Arquato is the birthplace of Illica, the librettist of Andrea Che-nier, and the monument a gift of Umberto Giordano, the composer.

I continued to write actively in my diary…. I defined LIFE as "a combination of dreams of the future and memories of the past", and I assumed that as one grew older the dreams would fade and the memories would play a larger role, and that one would start to wonder what might have been, if…However, these thoughts serve no purpose because LIFE is the only activity without a rehearsal; it is the real thing, and nobody can turn back. I also defined the PRESENT as that infinitesimal instant when the future becomes the past.

I also defined a lady as a woman who does not apologize, since her behavior does not require apologies, and a gentleman as a man who is never surprised since his knowledge and experience in life have made him aware of all possibilities.

On December 31st, 1940, summarizing the year, I wrote: "I believe that only by speaking one's mind and exchanging ideas, one will find a formula for the well being of the universe and for permanent peace. The well being of the world is founded on the well being of the people, and the well being of the people relies on the well being of the individual. When the individual will have found inner peace and will be able to provide for his or her needs, the entire world will be happy." I also wrote: "He who believes in himself is strong, he who believes in others is weak, and he who does not believe is wise".

I ended this entry with: "Good bye, year 1940! There is a war going on. I am considered a second, third rate citizen in my country. Year 1940. It has passed, like the millions of years that have preceded it. It had a different number to distinguish it from other years, but how many things have perhaps occurred in other years that were identical to the things that happened in 1940. One celebrates New Year's Eve. Instead of celebrating one should cry. Life is running out fast. I have not lived life yet, and it is already fleeing away, not ever to return. People believe in the eternity of the soul, in God, in the heavens, and eternal justice. Let them hope. Their disappointment will be greater when they shall realize that there is nothing beyond death. They will however never know it, because when they shall die, they will turn into nothing, and know nothing. People who believe in eternity are lucky, because they are living their lives with firm hope, and they will never find out that their faith and hope were only an illusion. At least I think it is. Could I be wrong?"

In April 1939, Italy invaded Albania and occupied it in a very short time. On October 28, 1940, Italy invaded Greece, Mussolini perhaps chose the 28th of October because on that day in 1922 his Fascist black shirts had marched on Rome, and King Victor Emanuel III had appointed him prime minister. This time, however, the date did not bring the same luck. The Italian army was held off by the Greek army. Hitler was unhappy with Mussolini's decision to attack Greece, and Great Britain promised support to Greece. Italy had lost Abyssinia, Eritrea and Somalia, and in North Africa was retreating in Libya.

I graduated from the "Liceo Scientifico" (the equivalent of high school) in 1942. Of course I was not allowed to enroll in an Italian University, and I was not interested in the parochial University in Milano where Drina was studying; I did not want to graduate in chemistry, I wanted to be a surgeon. I was confident that the war would end with the defeat of the Nazis and the Fascists, and that I would again become a regular member of society. I was able to enroll in medical school in Lausanne, Switzerland. In order to get there I needed a passport. I went to Rome for that purpose, but in spite of all the efforts, Jews were not issued passports by the Italian Government

On July 25th, 1943 when Mussolini was compelled by the Grand Fascist Council under the leadership of his son in law and foreign minister Galeazzo Ciano to hand over to King Victor Emanuel III the resignation of his cabinet, the King called upon General Badoglio to form a new Government That evening General Badoglio addressed the nation and the world on the radio.

There were very few German troops in Italy at that time. On July 10th, 1943 American and British troops had landed successfully in Sicily. The Italian armed forces and the country were fed up with the war. It would have been quite easy to block the Brenner Pass and disarm the few German soldiers that were in Italy at that time, and enter into quick peace negotiations with the Allies. Thousands of lives would have been saved, and great destruction and sorrow would have been avoided. The people were ready to surrender. Badoglio, however, made one irreparable mistake. In his short speech he said: "La guerra continua", war continues. This gave the German command time to pour thousands of soldiers into Italy, and de facto occupy the country when, on September 8th, 1943 Badoglio's Government concluded an armistice with the Allies.

Mussolini, who had bean imprisoned at the Gran Sasso since July 25th, 1943 was liberated by Scorzeni and a German commando unit and taken to Germany to meet Hitler. From there he returned to Northern Italy, formed a republican Government and started to rebuild the army and draft more men. King Victor Emanuel III and his Government fled to Brindisi in Southern Italy, which was occupied by Allied forces. The King, hoping to save the Monarchy, named his son Umberto regent, and the Italian Government declared war on Germany on October 13th, 1943. Mussolini tried and executed his son in law, former foreign minister Ciano and the other former members of the Fascist council who had voted against him. The country was in turmoil with the majority of the population terrorized by Fascist bands and German soldiers.

All this, and the tragedies and destructions caused by two years of war in Italy, could have been avoided had the King and Badoglio surrendered on July 25th, instead of speaking the three fatal words: "La guerra continua" (war continues).

On September 8th, 1943 it was the first time that I felt that my personal freedom and my life were threatened. German troops took over crossroads and major railroad centers, and my mother my sister and I felt that we should try and hide away from home. We wanted to take our Nonna with us, but she would not listen to us; she felt secure in her home!" Who is going to bother an old lady?" She said this over and over again. We did not have much time. We packed each one suitcase and left that evening on the last autobus for Trieste. The trains out of Fiume had been stopped. In Trieste we were able to take a train to Firenze.

We arrived in Firenze shortly after midnight. We had called Domenico Leoni, the owner of Villino Montebello from Trieste, and they were expecting us. As mentioned earlier, we had stayed there at other times, and we had befriended the owner. But this time was different: we had to stay there without being registered, and we all knew that Mr. Leoni was risking his life by agreeing to this arrangement He did not charge us one penny more than he was charging regular customers who were not hiding. Eventually he allowed not only the three of us to reside unregistered at the Villino Montebello, but also five cousins of ours and two friends from Fiume, all under the same terms.

The German troops entered Firenze on September 11th. The local Fascist organized a group named after their leader, Banda Carita', looking to arrest Jews and known political opponents.

Our I.D. cards from Fiume were stamped "di razza Ebraica" (of Jewish race), and we knew that we needed I.D. cards without that stamp, in case we were stopped in the street for any reason. Southern Italy had been bombed by the Allied air forces, and many people had fled their homes and had found shelter in Central and Northern Italy. A few days after settling in the Villino Montebello, my mother, sister and I had passport type pictures taken, and then went to Palazzo Vecchio, site of City Hall. We told the lady in charge of I.D. cards that we were refugees from Foggia and that we had lost our documents. We told her that our names were Carla, Anna and Enrico Carli, and that we needed I.D. cards. We also told her that we did not as yet have an address because we had not yet found accommodations. The employee did not ask any questions. I am sure that she realized from our accent that we had not lived in Southern Italy, but she also realized we needed help, and she was willing to help. She asked us to return the next day. When we went back the following day, we did not know whether we would find the police or the I.D. cards: we found the same lady and the I.D.

cards. No charge. Like the great majority of other Italians, this city employee helped quietly, discreetly and without asking any questions three strangers she would never see again in her life.

We were staying at the Villino Montebello without being registered, and we were eating our meals there. Food was rationed, however, and each resident was issued a bread card each month covering the food needs. Even in a restaurant one had to hand over a bread coupon in order to be served a meal. We had our September bread cards from Fiume with us when we arrived in Firenze, but we needed bread cards to eat in October and the following months. Not being registered as guests at the Villino Montebello, we could not have the City Hall of Firenze issue the necessary cards. On the first day of each month, for as long as we stayed in Firenze, I would go and visit a different suburb of Firenze (Peretola, Fucecchio, Careggi), give a different fictitious name and address, claiming to be a refugee from the South, and receive a ration card for myself, my mother and my sister.

In Fascist Italy things were not done efficiently, not even the persecutions. But when the Germans took over after September 8th, 1943, things changed, and Jews were systematically rounded up and taken to prisons and concentration camps. These persecutions, however, were tempered by the bonhomie of the Italian people, who in many instances, in contrast to the attitude of the German people toward the Jews, helped them to survive, putting sometimes their own lives at risk. This help was delivered at every level of the Italian society, showing that the twenty plus years of Fascist rule had not ruined the soul and good nature of the Italian people.

Aside from these dangerous situations and ever the possibility of being fingered and arrested either by the Fascist "Banda Carita'" or the Germans, our lives were progressing in an almost normal way. In the evenings we were listening with Mr. Leoni in his office to Radio London, hoping that the Allied advance would proceed rapidly, and that we would be liberated. This however was not to be. My position was further complicated by my age, 19, and the fact that I did not look either younger nor much older, that I was not disabled, and that 1 was not in uniform, which could only mean that I was either a Jew or a deserter, neither condition being enviable. During my stay in Firenze I was never stopped, nor was I asked this question.

Villino Montebello is located only a couple of blocks from the Teatro Comunale, the largest Theater and Opera House in Firenze, and the opera season was on its regular schedule. I attended many performances and many rehearsals. The tenor Aureliano Pertile, the soprano Ornella Rovero, and the conductor Argeo

Quadri stayed at the Villino Montebello when they were performing at the Comunale, and I had the opportunity to meet them and to befriend them.

Every few days we would call Nonna from different pay phones, so that the calls could not be traced, and ask her to leave home and to join us, but she would always decline with the same words: "who is going to harm an old lady?"

We were all hoping that the Allied forces would advance North from Southern Italy, and rid the country from the Germans and the Fascists. The Germans, however, had established a strong defensive line, the Gustav line, at the level of Monte Cassino and were offering a stubborn resistance. The British air force would occasionally raid Central Italy at night, and drop bombs on Florence trying to hit the railroad. During these air raids I would go up to the roof of the Villino Montebello and watch the flairs, the bombs and the antiaircraft tracers.

I am now translating directly from my diary. On December 7th, 1943 I wrote: "I am here in Firenze, not to study at the University, but as a fugitive, a refugee. I, too, am today in a situation of those men and women who years ago were fleeing the Hitlerian cruelty in Germany. At that time I did not understand them! Now my house is occupied by Germans, my belongings are scattered and my possessions have been confiscated by law. And I, a person, have to take refuge in a hospitable house to escape internment, synonym death! Things I was not capable of conceiving only a few weeks ago have become oppressing reality. Unfortunately, I am the oppressed! I am concerned not only about my physical situation, but also about my spiritual and emotional future. I am almost 20 years old; I am a man and I have to act as a man, I can not allow that the terror and slavery that Fascism and Nazism have imposed on me should guide my future to a life of renunciation, carried out with a bent back. If today it is impossible for me to live openly, I must prepare myself physically and emotionally to be ready to resume a normal life when the political situation will allow me to do it in bright sunlight".

On December 31st, 1943 I wrote: "Good bye 1943! Year full of happenings, perhaps a fatal year. The air raids have recently become more frequent, many times with large numbers of bombs being dropped. I go to the roof of the hotel and wait for the airplanes. I see them coming in close formations. I think about the crews. Who knows what those men are thinking? They come from far away, from across the ocean. They are Brits and Americans. What do they know about us? Nothing! Still at a certain moment, inexorably, they drop their mortal load. Many innocent people who a few seconds earlier were alive and well, are suddenly sprawled on dirt drenched in their own blood. And the crews are our friends! War is like a stupid children's game, only it is not a game, it is reality. Good-bye 1943! Perhaps one day, if I shall live to be old, I will have the courage to describe it in detail, and perhaps my tired soul will remember it with regret, in spite of all its horrors, remembering the age of 19".

Toward the end of January 1944 Mr. Leoni called us into his office. He was very upset. He informed us that the Germans had requisitioned half of the Villino Montebello in order to quarter some of their officers, and that they would move in sometime in February. Obviously this meant that we could not stay there any longer, and that he could not continue to keep us at the hotel. We thanked him for what he had done, and told him that we would look as soon as possible to another solution to our problem. The family had a meeting, and we decided that we would try to reach Switzerland. We had heard that it was possible to cross the border by hiring smugglers, and we decided to start by going to Milano. We knew that we could stay in Milano, at least for a few days, in the apartment where Drina had rented a room. We called Nonna again and told her about our plans, and asked her to join us in Milano. Her answer was still the same: "who is going to bother an old lady?" She also told us that the Germans had burned to the ground the Synagogue in Fiume. It would be the last time we ever talked to her.

Since my father's death my mother was receiving a very nice monthly pension from my Father's bank. After we left Fiume in September 1943, no money was coming in, and we were living by selling gold coins that we had brought with us. As I had mentioned earlier, my Father had always felt that in order to be reasonably safe, one should divide one's assets into three parts: cash and stocks, real estate, and gold and precious stones. This allowed us to survive financially. The real estate we owned in Fiume and the large vineyards we owned in Hungary did not do us any good.

My mother, Drina and I left Firenze on February 8th, 1944. Our cousins and the other friends from Fiume left separately. The train for Milano left at about 9 PM. It was full. There were civilians, soldiers, and men in Fascist uniform. We stood in the corridor, next to our suitcases. When we arrived in Bologna we found that that railroad station had been destroyed by Allied bombers. We left the train south of the station and walked with our luggage for a long stretch to a train north of the station going to Milano. This train pulled into the railroad station in Milano around 5 AM. Mother, Drina and I went with our luggage into a large waiting room packed with people. There was a curfew in Milano from 10 PM to 7 AM and passengers could not leave the station during that period of time. We found a small area where we could sit on the floor; leaning against our luggage. There were people of all ages in that room, including children, some awake, and some asleep on the floor. There were also a few German soldiers with rifles walking around. We were waiting for 7 o'clock to come around, so that we could leave and go to Mrs. Andrei's apartment on the third floor of Corso Sempione 6.

Around 6: 30 I needed to go to the bathroom. I got up and slowly walked to the corner of the waiting room, where the bathrooms were. Suddenly I felt the nozzle of a gun in my back and a fairly deep male voice saying: "Dokumente". I did not expect this. I looked at the people in the waiting room, and all eyes seemed to be pointing at me. I had two sets of ID. cards, my regular one stating that I was a Jew, and the one that I had gotten in Firenze, which stated that I was Enrico Carli, and not "di razza ebraica". One was in my left side pocket, and the other one, the real one, in the right inside pocket. I mentally debated for a few seconds which one to present; my real one was definitely bad, the other one would have required an explanation why I was not in uniform. The same voice repeated: "Dokumente!", louder this time. Almost at the same moment the sirens announcing an air raid went off, causing a pandemonium, with people running all over for shelter. Whoever had pointed the gun at my back disappeared. Mother and Drina also went for shelter, and I locked myself in the bathroom until 7 AM, when the curfew was over, the air raid had finished, and we were able to leave the railroad station and take tram # 1 to the apartment.

Mrs. Andrei received us with open arms. We told her that we would leave as soon as we would be able to find a way to get to Switzerland, and to our surprise and joy she informed us that she had heard from a friend of hers, a German Lutheran Minister, Father Wabnitz, that there were smugglers able to guide people out of Italy to Switzerland. That same evening she made arrangements for me to meet the head smuggler in a bar. We informed our cousins, and we met at the specified bar. The requested price was 20.000 Lire (at that time the equivalent of about 2,000 dollars) per person, and it was decided to meet the following evening at 7PM at the railroad station in Como. We would be a group of eleven people. I was the youngest at 19, and my cousin's father the oldest at 65. The agreement called for leaving the money with Mrs. Andrei. The smugglers would get a sign from us to take to Mrs. Andrei, after they had taken us across the border. The sign, unknown to the smugglers, was one half of a five Lire note; the numbers on the two halves had to match.

There were eight smugglers at the railroad station in Como. The eleven of us had left Milano around five o'clock. Each one of us had one suitcase, and the smugglers would be carrying the suitcases. We started to walk in groups of two and three. I was carrying a small yellow suitcase. It was quite heavy, but I would not let anybody touch it. It contained about one thousand gold coins, and represented our entire worldly possessions.

It was dark, it was cold, and we were quiet. We walked across the city in a western direction, rather slowly, but with a steady gait, the smugglers carrying the bags, and intermingling with us. It was dark, and we walked in silence. Nobody was talking. The direction was toward the hill of Brunate. We climbed the hill, and on the way down we stopped for about 10 minutes. It was about 1 o'clock in the morning. We continued our walk up and down another taller hill. It was cold and dark, a moonless night.

A little after 5 o'clock in the morning we stopped again, and the head smuggler said: "We are in Switzerland, we will leave you here, and we will return to Milano. Give me the sign to take to Mrs. Andrei". We handed him the half 5 Lire note, and thanked him profusely. They dropped the suitcases and promptly disappeared. We sat down waiting for the first light of the morning.

At about 6 o'clock we noticed two silhouettes that could have been soldiers walking in the valley about 500 yards from us. We called to them. They were Swiss soldiers on patrol. We asked them to help us with the luggage. Their answer was: "You are still in Italy, we can not come over there, the border is down here". We moved as fast as we could to where the Swiss guards were, thanking the good fortune that we had not been seen by an Italian or German patrol while we were waiting for the morning to arrive.

VI

We were escorted to a Swiss Guard station and interrogated by an officer. We were immediately asked if we had any means of subsistence. My cousins had done business in Chiasso, and had a checking account there. I opened my small yellow suitcase and showed the officer our gold coins. I was told that they had to be deposited with the Swiss Volksbank, and that they would be sold by the bank to provide us with Swiss francs, as we needed them. I learned later that some refugees, who had no means of subsistence, would be refused asylum.

The whole group of us was then transferred to the nearby quarantine camp of Balerna. Upon arrival in Balerna, we had a hot shower, and we were "deloused". There were two large rooms, one for men and one for women, with straw on the ground to sleep on. Each of us was assigned a responsibility, either in the kitchen or in the cleaning department. I was assigned to the kitchen to peel potatoes. We met other refugees there, about 30 altogether, and we were told that the quarantine would last about three weeks.

Drina developed a high fever and an acute tonsillitis. In 1944 antibiotics did not exist in Switzerland. Within a few days she was found to have an acute nephritis. She was hospitalized in the Cantonal Hospital in Mendrisio, but in spite of every treatment available at that time, she developed kidney failure, and died peacefully a few days later. She was buried in Lugano. My mother was devastated.

A few days later my Mother and I were informed that we could leave the camp in Balerna. We decided to go to Geneva, where we settled in a small apartment in Rue Bonivard 12.

A few days after we arrived in Geneva, I was able to enroll in Medical School at the University of Geneva, and to start attending classes. It helped very much that I spoke the language fluently thanks to our French governess. It was the first time since the racial laws of 1938 that I was able to frequent a regular school and to intermingle with other students as an equal. Most of the students were Swiss nationals, but there were also foreign students, some of them refugees, Jewish and Christian, some civilian and some military. There was a contingent of Italian officers and soldiers, who had deserted and crossed the border into Switzerland.

Among them there were two students at the School of Music, who would become quite famous in their field after the war: the pianist Orazio Frugoni, and the tenor Giuseppe di Stefano.

The relationship among all the students was cordial. Between spring and fall quarters all the male Swiss students would serve in the Swiss Army Reserve, and the male foreign students would be required to go to work camps. I spent one month on Iffigenalp with about twenty other students removing rocks and pebbles from mountain pastures, so that the cows could graze without getting injured. We would work about 10 hours a day, receive one large bowl of potato soup, a loaf of bread and sleep on straw in tents. We worked seven days a week, and we were isolated from the surrounding population. The camaraderie was great, and we essentially enjoyed what we were doing. We were paid 30 cents a day. After Iffigenalp I was sent to Champery to work as a lumberjack. The routine was the same, but we worked only six days a week, and we were allowed to leave the camp on Sundays, and walk to a nearby village if we desired. All the young men were treated the same, regardless of ethnic or religious background. After my work at Champery ended, I returned to Geneva for the beginning of the fall quarter. My mother and I moved from Rue Bonivard 12 to Rue du Vieux College 7. This apartment was closer to the University and shortened my walk to and from school.

Many years later, in February of 1998, Rabbi Marvin Hier of the Simon Wiesenthal Center in Los Angeles wrote a fundraising letter, and mentioned discrimination against Jews in the Swiss labor camps. I wrote him the following letter:

"I have read your form letter about the Swiss labor camps, and your pledge card which starts: ""Yes I am shocked..."" I was shocked at the tone of your letter. It does contain some truth, but it exaggerates the negatives and minimizes the positives, and contains statements that are at least questionable. I know, I was there. I am one of the survivors as a refugee in Switzerland. I spent time in two labor camps: Iffigenalp and Champery. Yes, we did sleep on straw mattresses, and yes, we ate mainly potato soup, but we Jews were not singled out. Jews and Christians were treated alike. During the summer the Swiss boys served in the Army Reserve, the refugee boys served in labor camps. There were no barbwires, there were no armed guards. We were free to come and go, but there was no place to go. We were clearing meadows or working as lumberjacks on the sides of mountains. I had sufficient assets (gold coins) that I brought with me when I entered Switzerland to take care of my needs. I did not need help, nor did I receive help from any relief organization. During the school year I was living in Geneva and going to Medical School. During vacations I had to work in a labor camp. I do believe however, that the Swiss did take advantage of me when they exchanged my gold coins, at a rate determined by the Swiss bank. I have asked the Holocaust claims processing office of the State of New York Banking Dept. to look into it. I wonder if you might have any comment on this subject. It is very easy to be sanctimonious fifty tears later. But is it fair? We all make mistakes and hindsight always has 20/20 vision. I was able to walk across the Alps, get to Switzerland, was accepted as a refugee, and I survived, My grandmother stayed home, was taken to a concentration camp, and perished in an oven I am grateful for my life, and I can overtook the straw mattress and the potato soup". To this day my letter has remained unanswered.

Among the refugees in Geneva there was Dr. Mario Donati who had been Professor of surgery at the University of Milano until he was removed in 1938 following the racial laws, He would sit in on the examinations of the students who were planning to return to Italy after the war, and suggest a grade according to the scores used in Italian Universities, 18 being the minimum passing score, and 30 being the best possible score.

On June 4th, 1944 the Allied troops had liberated Rome. On June 6th, 1944 the Allied forces had landed in France. The war seemed to have turned in a very positive way. News in Switzerland, both in the newspapers and on the radio, was quite succinct. We were listening to radio London trying to interpret some of those cryptic messages, and trying to maintain our optimism. Some rumors started to circulate at this time about "labor camps" in Germany bordering on horror stories, but these were only rumors, devoid of fact or details. It was only after the war had ended that the real facts, horrendous as they were, became known. Since the war had started, I had always felt that Nazi Germany and fascist Italy would be defeated. Even after France had fallen, and London was under continuous air attacks, I felt that Britain and her Allies would prevail. Now that the Allies had landed in France, the successful end of the war seemed so much closer.

As I have stated earlier, Life is a sequence of dreams for the future and memories of the past, and I was trying to forget the past and think of a bright future. School was fun, and I enjoyed going to classes and study. I can only say again how grateful I was to my parents for giving me the opportunity of having a French governess when I was a child. The lessons and the examinations at the University of course were in French, and my social life would have been different had I not spoken the language.

The bank where we had been told to deposit our gold coins changed the coins into Swiss francs at a rate, which was quite below the open market rate, and provided us with a sufficient amount of money to live from month to month. The few luxuries I allowed myself were the concerts of the Swiss Romand orchestra and Chamber concerts. Wilhelm Backhaus would perform every Thursday during the winter months, until he had completed all of Beethoven's piano sonatas.

In August the Allied forces entered Paris. In September they entered Brussels. In Geneva we were wondering if the German troops, retreating from France and Northern Italy, would eventually cross into Switzerland. This did not happen, and we continued our daily routine at the University. It was obvious that the end of the war was nearing, and we started to think about life after the war. What had happened to our home? Would we be able to return? What had happened to our family and friends? Had they survived? Had they saved themselves?

News from German occupied Europe was somehow filtering into Switzerland. My mother and I were told that my father's oldest brother Vilmos {William), who had been a member of Parliament in Hungary in the 1920's, had committed suicide when the Germans entered Hungary. We found out after the war that unfortunately this rumor was true.

In March 1945 I took my first exam: Anatomy. I passed with a mark of 30, the highest possible mark. Shortly thereafter I passed Chemistry and Biology. I was on the road of becoming a Doctor of Medicine. As a student I participated in the activities offered by the University and by student organizations; my participation was limited only by the amount of money available. The opportunities and the friendships were unlimited.

President Roosevelt died of natural causes on the 12th of April 1945 in Warm Springs, Georgia. Mussolini was captured and killed by Italian Partisans on April 28th, 1945, while attempting to escape to Switzerland. Hitler committed suicide in his bunker in Berlin on April 30th, 1945. On May 8th, 1945 the war in Europe ended with the surrender of the German army.

It seemed like the end of a long nightmare. A new nightmare was about to begin: the return "home". What home? Where? What were we going to find? Were relatives and friends alive? What had happened to our properties? First, however, I was going to finish the school year and take the exams.

Word came that the Jews of Fiume had been deported in early 1944. My Nonna among them. The rumor was that she had died in the gas chambers of the Risiera San Sabba in Trieste. Unfortunately this proved to be true.

At the end of the war the Yugoslav partisans of Tito had overrun and occupied Fiume.

In July of 1945 the Potsdam conference convened. This conference decided the fate of millions of people and their properties. The devastating outcome was due to the fact that the Soviet Union was represented by a ruthless and experienced dictator, Stalin, and the Western powers by the then inexperienced President Truman, and the newly elected and equally inexperienced Prime Minister Attlee. With the "atomic bomb" ace in his hand, President Truman did not take advantage of this trump card. He and his advisors were more interested in saving the industrial complex of West Germany, and in getting the Soviet Union to declare war on Japan than in settling the future of the Central and Eastern European society in a fair and just manner. I have wondered many times if the Soviet Union would have been allowed to dominate Eastern Europe, and if my hometown of Fiume would have been given to communist Yugoslavia had President Roosevelt not died, and had Prime Minister Churchill not lost his reelection. But we will never know, since, as I have previously stated, life does not have a rehearsal, it is the real thing, and the only thing.

Croatia did not deserve to be rewarded. The Croatian Ustase Government had willingly collaborated with Nazi Germany and persecuted the Serbs and the Jews, sending them to concentration camps and murdering them. At the same time officers of the Italian army stationed in Yugoslavia were trying to protect the Serbs and the Jews against the specific orders of the Ustase regime. At the end of the war, however, Ante Pavelic and the other Ustase leaders were able to find refuge in Argentina and escape just retribution with help from the Vatican, and under the protection of Pope Pius XII.

This Pope, who had never spoken out against the German atrocities, did not lift one finger nor utter one word when, on October 16th, 1943 the Nazis rounded up and sent to the death camps 1,259 Roman Jews whose ancestors had lived in Rome over twenty centuries. After the war, however, he made it possible for many Nazis from Germany and other parts of Europe to use the Vatican to escape to South America. He certainly did not deserve to be addressed "your Holiness."

Before leaving Geneva, I felt the need to express my feeling about my stay in this city. Among the students in my class there was a beautiful young lady, Éliane Dominicé, whose beauty and demeanor I admired...We were friends, but we had never dated, I wrote her the following letter: "Leaving Geneva, perhaps never to return, I feel the need to express myself and to write to someone in my class of whom at least I know the name. Shoved by the tempest, which is convulsing the world, I found myself in Geneva, the magnificent Geneva, surrounded by quiet, by peace, by study and by youth. And today, torn again by a whirlwind, I am leaving, perhaps never to return. This parenthesis of carefree University life has come to an end, and the next one will probably open in Italy. I shall never see Chodat, Weiglé, Guyenot and Meyer look at me and talk to me from their chair. I shall not see again the well-known faces of my classmates; I shall not see again "my" old University. It is strange that I should consider all these things as "mine", as if I were jealous of this world, I, who essentially have been only a wondering foreigner, a refugee. And yet, strangely enough, I felt very much at home in Geneva, and it seemed to me that I had not been here only a few months, but forever. I thought of all this during the Zofingue party. I realized then that in the old Europe, tortured by deep mourning and torn to shreds by grudges, there was a bunch of young people, a bunch of students, who had remained outside of all conflicts, who had remained the custodians of the beautiful University traditions, while the rest of the world's youth slaughtered each other horribly. A youth in Geneva had written on a banner the word AMITIE (Friendship), the most beautiful among all words, the symbol and the synthesis of civilization. That evening I was truly sorry not to be one of "you". Today I do hope that, when serenity will have returned to the rest of Europe, the word friendship will become the bond among all of the young people, a sincere bond that will bring them all together" I never mailed the letter; I was not sure it would be understood.

After the school year and the exams were finished successfully, my mother and I decided to leave Geneva in July, and to return. Return to where? News in the press and on the radio about Fiume were disconcerting. We decided to return to Firenze. The "return" actually meant a new beginning, it meant to set new goals, to set a sound foundation in order to be able to realize the old dreams made impossible by the racial laws, the war, the persecutions. To find again peace, serenity and tranquility, and to forget the horrors of the past. To return to a "normal life". Leaving Switzerland meant the end to a "temporary life", and settling in Firenze would mean the beginning of a "permanent life". First we would have to make sure that we have the means to live while I complete my studies and put myself in a position of earning a living.

I had always felt that there were two ways of living a life: from day to day enjoying the small joys life can offer, or to live with a well stated goal, as a true man, aware of his duties, responsibilities and of his rights. Circumstances had compelled me to live from day to day, and I had been lucky to survive. Now the true "LIFE" was beginning, and I wanted to follow the examples of those great men who through their accomplishments and moral behavior had gained the respect of the future generations, and perhaps achieve the honor of serving as an example to others.

VII

We returned to Firenze at the end of July, and came back to the Villino Montebello and Mr. Leoni. The retreating German army had blown up all the bridges across the river Arno, with the exception of Ponte Vecchio, where they had demolished all the houses on both sides of the bridge to prevent the use of it. I contacted the University of Firenze, where I had not been allowed to set foot during the racial laws, and submitted my curriculum from the University of Geneva and the results of the examinations I had taken, and I requested admission to the fourth year in the School of Medicine, where I would have been had the racial laws not existed. I was first granted admission to the third year, but eventually I was admitted to the fourth year; it was up to me to attend all the required courses, and to pass the exams.

Sad news was piling up. Yes, my grandmother had been deported and had died. My mother's sister and her husband had been taken to Auschwitz and never returned. My father's two sisters and their husbands and two little cousins of mine were also assassinated in Auschwitz. My father's youngest brother, who had been Director of Shell in Budapest, also died in Auschwitz. The vineyards in Hungary, about 6000 acres, that had been in the family for 200 years, had been expropriated by the Hungarian Nazis. All the horrors of the German concentration camps became known, though it took a while to understand the immensity and the tragedy of those crimes. Many people found it very difficult if not impossible to believe in a just Deity that might have allowed the carrying out of such atrocities. I certainly felt that if ever there was a God, He or She truly died in Auschwitz. After the Lisbon earthquake of 1755 Voltaire wrote Candide to question the view that God presides over the best of all possible worlds, and that all is for the best.

Mother went to Fiume to find out about our home. She returned a few days later with some of the furniture. The silver and china and most of the linen had been taken by the Germans and the local fascists. Grandmother's house had been destroyed during a bombing raid. Our home was occupied by Croats who had come to town with Tito. Most of the local population had left town when Marshal Tito's forces occupied it. The picture was bleak. There was no hope for my

Mother to receive again her pension from my Father's bank: the bank did not exist any more. My father's foresight to have one third of our assets in gold and other precious metals allowed us to survive. We moved to a small apartment in via della Robbia 23 in Firenze, determined to live our lives not by mourning the past, but by doing the best we could into the future.

The International Military Tribunal established in Nurenberg ruled that an individual's obedience to orders for having committed acts against humanity and for having committed war crimes is not a defense for having committed such acts. In 1996 Daniel Jonah Goldhagen will publish a book "Hitler's willing executioners".

Victor Emanuel III, King of Italy, tried to save the Monarchy by abdicating in favor of his son Umberto. It did not help. On June 2nd, 1946 a referendum produced a majority in favor of a Republic. It was one vote I very much enjoyed casting. It was a fairly close vote. Many men and women in Italy were still dreaming of "the good old days".

On October 15th, 1945 I took my first examination at the University of Firenze. It was biological chemistry, the Professor was Simonelli and the grade 26 out of a possible 30. I was informed at this time that I would be admitted to the fourth year. I realized that I could graduate from Medical School in July 1948, provided I could pass all the required examinations.

Little by little I would also settle into a social life. The other students had been together for a number of years, and I was the outsider. But this did not last for any length of time, and the friendships developed progressively. I wanted to spend more time in the surgical department, and I went to see Dr. Pietro Valdoni, the Professor of Surgery at his home to ask him if I could extern in his department trying to learn the basics of the profession. The Associate Professor was Gaetano Gentile, the son of the philosopher Giovanni Gentile, who had been murdered in Firenze during the war. Professor Gentile and I became friends, and I have always been and I shall always be thankful for his teachings and for his friendship. I had lived in Firenze before, but walking the streets of this beautiful city now had a different feeling. I did not have to look around any longer wondering if somebody would stop me, question me, arrest me or even deport me. I was like anybody else, and I could admire the beautiful buildings and monuments without second thoughts.

Among the sites I enjoyed most visiting were the Uffizi Gallery, and the Church of Santa Croce. The Uffizi Gallery shows statues of many distinguished sons of Firenze, among them Galileo Galilei, Cosimo the Elder, Giotto, Amerigo Vespucci, Niccolo' Macchiavelli, Michelangelo, Leonardo da Vinci, Donatello,

Benvenuto Cellini, Dante Alighieri, Francesco Petrarca, Giovanni Boccaccio, Lorenzo il Magnifico. Many years later my son Ned, who is a great sports fan, looking at these monuments turned to me and said: "Dad, this is the Florence Hall of Fame". Hall of Fame indeed! It is certainly a coincidence that Lorenzo il Magnifico, the great Patron of the Renaissance died in 1492, the year the "New World" was discovered.

Near this illustrious "Hall of Fame", in Piazza della Signoria, not far from the entrance to Palazzo Vecchio, there is an oval plaque in the ground with this inscription: "Qui dove con i suoi confratelli Fra Domenico Buonvicini e Fra Silvestro Maruffi il 23 Maggio 1498 per iniqua sentenza fu impiccato ed arso Fra Girolamo Savonarola dopo quattro secoli fu collocata questa memoria". (This plaque was placed here four centuries after Fra Girolamo Savonarola and his brothers Fra Domenico Buonvicini and Fra Silvestro Maruffi were hanged and burned at the stake on this place on May 23rd, 1498 because of a wicked sentence). It almost seems inconsistent to have within a very short walking distance the tributes to the Great Men of the Renaissance and the memory of a brutal execution by a fundamentalist religious tribunal.

An Italian poet of the XIX century, Ugo Foscolo, whom I like to call the Italian Lord Byron, wrote a poem "I Sepolcri" (The Tombs). In that poem he describes the Church of Santa Croce and the many illustrious men who are buried there, Michelangelo, Rossini, Macchiavelli, Galileo among them. The Catholic Church had considered Galileo a "heretic" and had kept him prisoner for many years in the Torre del Gallo. The Torre del Gallo in 1945 housed the Department of Physics of the University of Florence. I took my physic's exam in the room in which Galileo had been kept prisoner. I frequented classes regularly, spent a great deal of time in the Department of Surgery, scrubbing occasionally as second assistant, and took my examinations when I had qualified for them. Pretty soon I caught up with the time I had missed, and became current.

At that time Italian Universities did not have fraternities or sororities, unlike the good old Zofingen at the "uni" in Geneva. There were no dormitories. Students lived at home with their parents or other relatives, or they rented a room somewhere in town. Therefore there was no "organized" social life. Get togethers and parties were called for by friends and schoolmates.

The Italian Governments did not last long, but were essentially Center Right, and headed by Alcide De Gasperi, member of the "Democrazia Cristiana", the largest party in Parliament. It would remain that way for many years. My tendencies were more to the left, but somehow the Social Democrats could not get enough representatives to play an influential role. The Communist party was strong, but too extreme to justify support from the Middle Class. Many former Fascists traded their black shirts in for a red shirt, others supported the far right Neo Fascist group. Fair-minded people would never consider guilt by association. The racial laws were the most blatant example of guilt by association. When time came to square the accounts, the culprits were not treated the same way, though it would have been good to give them a taste of their own medicine. Former active members of the Fascist party were reabsorbed into society, and their past deeds or misdeeds closed under the heading of "patriotism". Mussolini's son Romano was allowed to pursue a successful career as a jazz musician, and Mussolini's granddaughter Alessandra was allowed to pursue a political career, She was actually elected to Parliament as a member of the far right neo-fascist party.

On February 10th, 1947 the peace treaties were signed in Paris. Fiume and most of the former Venezia Giulia, and the islands of the Adriatic, and Zara were annexed to Yugoslavia. Another chapter of my life had been closed, and another decision by inept or misinformed politicians had changed and mainly ruined the lives of hundreds of thousands of innocent individuals.

On September 30th, 1946 the Nurenberg trial ended with 12 death sentences. Tens of thousands of Hitler's "willing executioners," however, were reabsorbed into the general population and never paid for their crimes. The Allies were quite concerned about the presence of the Soviet Union in Eastern and Central Europe and wanted a viable Germany to serve as a buffer. The adoption of the "Marshall Plan" in 1948 was prompted not only by humanitarian reasons, but also by practical political reasons.

I continued to attend classes and take exams when they were due. In my spare time I would work in the Department of Surgery. The professor rewarded my interest by allowing me to do an appendectomy on May 12th, 1947. The professor acted as first assistant. I considered myself the youngest surgeon in Italy. Today it would be unthinkable to have a student perform any kind of surgery considering the antagonistic attitude of patients toward doctors, and the malpractice suit climate. My patient did very well and she was discharged a few days later. She was never told that a student had taken out her appendix.

A peculiar attitude appeared among some orthodox rabbis who had survived the Holocaust. They were taking the lead from Rabbi Hayim Elazar Shapira from Slovakia, who in 1933, shortly after the Nazis had posted guards in front of Jewish owned stores in Gennany to prevent customers from entering the stores and purchase merchandise from Jews, stated that these guards were carrying out God's wish to punish the merchants for not keeping the Sabbath. Another Rabbi, Yoel Teitelbaum of Satmar, argued that God had sent the Holocaust to punish the Zionist Jews who wanted to settle in Israel without waiting for the Messiah, and therefore acting against God's wishes. These statements only prove that Jewish fundamentalism is just as misguided, arrogant, destructive and pernicious as that of any other persuasion or denomination.

The bloodiest war in human history had barely finished, and new clouds were gathering on the horizon. Berlin was isolated by Soviet troops, and an airlift had to be established. Churchill's "iron curtain" had arisen. President Roosevelt had envisioned a new fraternity of nations with the creation of the United Nations, and had advocated the end of all colonialism. Unfortunately he had overestimated the will and the capacity of the people in the former colonies to govern themselves in freedom and respect for their neighbors. Former colonies fell under monarchic or military dictatorships, and Middle Eastern and African countries plundered and fought each other, guided by self-proclaimed military rulers or by religious fanatics. The decolonization of under developed countries produced mainly the assumption of power by dictators who enslaved their people for personal gain. From Libya to Iraq to Syria to Central Africa, people were slaughtered and poverty and disease spread. I believe the continuation of a benign colonial rule would have been much more beneficial to those populations until education and work ethic had become more generalized, and democracy and self rule better understood so that they would have been able to administer it. Roosevelt meant well by proclaiming the end to colonialism, but he forgot that the American colonies, when they rebelled and proclaimed freedom, were populated by people with the same traditions and education as their European brothers and sisters, while the inhabitants of Africa and the Middle East did not have the same background and neither the will nor the capacity for self rule. During all these upheavals, I completed the required courses, passed the exams, and graduated from Medical School on July 28th, 1948 with 108 points out of a possible 110. My thesis "Changes in the Nucleic Acid caused by X-rays in the Skin of Guinea Pigs" won first prize.

VIII

Doctor Valdoni had been appointed Professor of Surgery at the University of Rome, and he asked me to join his staff. The post-graduate training in Italy at that time was different from the residency program in the United States. In the United States the training programs are well defined in time and scope while in Italy there was no specified time to be spent training. One joined a professor's staff at his invitation, and one did the work assigned by him, until, in his opinion, one was ready for an examination. It was a very arbitrary and capricious system, and one's future depended on the professor's judgment, and sometimes, whim. Professor Valdoni liked me, and he gave me many opportunities in research as well as clinical work. He made it also possible for me to work in vascular surgery, which at the time was in its infancy. I published a number of papers: "Anesthesia for Peroral Endoscopies", "Bronchial Healing using various different suture materials following pneumonectomy in dogs", "Treatment of marginal peptic ulcers following partial gastric resection", "Emergency lobectomy for bleeding congenital cyst of the lung", "Treatment of echinococcus cysts of the liver and of the lung". and more.

Rome is the only capital city in the world with double embassies: Embassy to the Republic of Italy, and Embassy to the Vatican. The diplomatic social life is twice as busy as in other capitals, and eligible bachelors are quite popular on the guest lists. I had a very busy schedule in the Department of Surgery of the University of Rome, but during my infrequent evenings off I was a welcome guest at parties of a number of Embassies. I would also occasionally spend time with friends playing bridge. Tito Gobbi, world famous baritone, would play bridge in the same group when he was in Rome and was not performing. We became friends.

In spite of the progress I was making, and in spite of the fact that most of my colleagues considered me certain to have a successful career, I was apprehensive about my future. Mother and I were running out of money. She had lost her pension and her possessions, and had always taken care of me. I felt responsible for her. I did not want to do general practice, and I did not know how long it would take to complete my surgical training and be able to earn a living in that field. It was also disturbing to me to see a number of people who had strongly supported the old fascist regime go about their business undisturbed. None of the Italian Governments that followed the fall of Mussolini had mentioned compensation for the losses suffered by Italian Jews because of the racial laws. In fact, none of these governments even offered an apology for the discrimination, persecution, and damages caused by these laws.

The thought of leaving Italy and starting a new life began to surface. During one of the various embassy parties I had met an official of the Australian Embassy, and I had been assured that I would have been issued a visa upon request. Australia, however, seemed so far away, and I could not bring myself to go "that far". I also found out through an acquaintance at the American Embassy that quotas had been increased for a number of professional categories, and that I would qualify.

In April 1951 Professor Valdoni and I went to a surgical conference in Montecatini, where I was to give a paper. Returning to Rome in his car, he was driving and I was sitting in the front seat next to him. We were alone. I started to talk, and I said that I had always appreciated very much all the help and the opportunities he had given me, and that I was very grateful to him for all he had done for me, but that I did not have the luxury to wait for things to happen, and that I was thinking about going to the United States and starting a new life. There was a short silence while he continued to drive, and then Professor Valdoni said: "If I were in your shoes, I would do the same". I felt relieved. The last thing I wanted to do was to hurt his feelings.

The next morning I called my mother in Florence, and told her that I was going to the United States. She said immediately, "I am going with you". My mother had a brother, uncle Ernest, who lived in New York City, and whom I had never met. He had served in the army in World War I, and shortly after the end of the war, he had returned home to Fiume. But after his return, he had had a very strong argument with his father (Nonna's husband) about a dog. He had resented the argument so much, that he left home and emigrated to the United States. He did not contact the family for a very long time, and then only occasionally, He never married, and he worked as a maitred' in a fine restaurant in New York City. Mother contacted him and told him that we would be coming to New York. He offered us hospitality.

We got our visas after passing a physical examination with negative skin tests for tuberculosis. Mother sold most of the furniture, shipping only the things that were especially dear to her, including a portrait of my father and a portrait of my sister. Admiral Nino Bisconti, who commanded the port of Naples, and who many years earlier had commanded the port of Fiume and had there married Helen Kiss, the daughter of the cashier in my father's bank, accompanied us aboard the "Vulcania", the ship that would take us to New York. My father had been best man at their wedding.

We arrived in New York on July 10th, 1951, and uncle Ernest met us at the pier, and took us to his home.

IX

I knew two hospitals in New York through the literature: Columbia-Presbyterian Medical Center, and Mount Sinai Hospital. On July 11th I went to Presbyterian Hospital and asked to speak to the Professor of Surgery. He was busy, but his associate Dr. David Habif was kind enough to receive me. We talked for a couple of hours, and he explained to me that in order to be eligible to take my surgical specialty boards I would have to go through a residency program, but that the programs started either July 1st or January 1st. Then he looked at me and asked: "Did you graduate first in your class?" I said: "No, probably top 10%, but not first". He laughed and said: "You must be an honest man, because every foreign student I ever interviewed graduated first in his class. You know more about vascular surgery than I do, and I did not know if you were just bullshitting me or telling me the truth, but since you are an honest man, I believe you. I can offer you a Fellowship in vascular surgery starting tomorrow morning at 7 o'clock. You will be working with Doctor Blakemore. The stipend is 200 dollars a month".

For years to come I have felt so lucky not to have graduated first in my class. Had I done so, I would probably not have gotten the job at Columbia. Dr. Habif would have thought that I was embellishing my story like all the other foreign graduates he had interviewed.

That afternoon we rented an apartment in Forest Hills, and moved in. The next morning I went to work at Presbyterian Hospital, Our life in the New World had begun.

Doctor Blakemore was a very well known surgeon who had devised the porta-caval shunt for portal hypertension. He was also interested in aortic aneurysms and had devised a procedure of rubber banding, wiring and coagulating the aneurysms, which was later replaced by grafting. He scheduled a porta-caval shunt every Tuesday and an aneurysm of the aorta every Saturday. I would assist in surgery and also check the pressures in the vessels before, during, and after surgery through catheters placed in the vessels and connected to a machine affectionally called the "green monster".

Day by day and week by week, life became more "normal". A social life developed involving people met at work at the Hospital, neighbors, and Italian Jewish emigrees who had come to New York after the racial laws were enacted in Italy, and before Italy had entered World War II. I was having lunch one day at the Hospital with a surgical resident who was also working with the "green monster", Doctor Hugh Fitzpatrick from Omaha, Nebraska, and I expressed my admiration for the United States, for the hospitality, and for the way of life. He looked at me and smilingly said: "How would you know? You have not been there yet; the United States starts west of the Hudson River." It took me many years to understand what that statement meant.

I had kept in touch with Professor Valdoni in Rome, keeping him informed of my activities. In January 1952, he was awarded Honorary Membership in the American College of Surgeons, and he came to the United States to attend a meeting of the American College of Surgeons in Chicago, It was a very proud moment for me to pick him up at the airport in New York, take him to Presbyterian Hospital and introduce him to Doctor Georges H. Humphries, Professor of Surgery at Columbia University. By the way, Doctor Humphries and I presented a paper at that meeting in Chicago on open chest massage of the heart for cardiac arrest.

I went for a few days to Maine to take the examination for a license to practice medicine, and I passed the examination. The reason I went to Maine was that the State of Maine reciprocated with every State of the Union except Florida and California.

In order to be able to take the examinations for the American Board of Surgery, I needed to be accepted in a surgical residency program. Residencies did not pay much in those days, and I needed enough money to provide for my mother and myself. Doctor Habif introduced me to Doctor Rousselot, Director of Surgery at Saint Vincent's Hospital, affiliated with New York University, and he accepted me in that residency program and gave me credit for some of my previous experience. He also made it possible for me to get a grant from the U.S. Navy to do research in peripheral vascular diseases. This arrangement provided a sufficient amount of money for our needs. I started work at St. Vincent's Hospital on July 1st, 1952, and I spent two years in that institution. The first paper I published there" Arteriography in the diagnosis, prognosis, and treatment of arterial diseases of the lower extremity" won first prize for best paper by a resident from a Hospital in the State of New York.

Those were the days of Senator McCarthy and red baiting. Anyone who disagreed with his views was labeled a "communist". I was watching the Senate hearings on television, and was sadly reminded of the fascist days in Italy when "Il Duce ha sempre ragione" (The Duce is always right) was plastered on walls and buildings all over Italy. I found out, however, that there was one big difference: in fascist Italy public opinion was controlled by the Government, while in the United States the press, radio and television were free to show Senator McCarthy's true colors, causing him eventually to lose his power, even if he lost it only after he had done a great deal of harm. It was Democracy in action in a free society, a great lesson and a new experience for me.

Many years later, at the beginning of the 21st century, there will be again indications of excesses in the political arena, this time "communists" being replaced by "terrorists" and Senator McCarthy being replaced by other politicians.

Chemotherapy was starting to become more proficient in treating some forms of cancer, organ transplants were being initiated with primary emphasis on kidney transplants, and the heart lung machine was being perfected, allowing the performance of open-heart surgery. If kidney dialysis and kidney transplants had been available ten years earlier, my sister might not have had to die.

Those were also the days preceding the malpractice mania. The members of the attending staff would discuss openly with the resident staff errors in diagnosis, errors in management and errors in technique whenever they occurred. This was a good way to teach and to learn. Today one would be considered very foolish to mention them. Doing so would be an open invitation to start a malpractice lawsuit. Those were also the days when hospital administrators were called just that, administrators, while today they are all powerful CEO's, paid way out of proportion of their worth.

After completing my senior residency at St. Vincent's Hospital, I returned to Presbyterian Hospital to work with Doctor Habif trying to solve the problem of swelling of the arm following radical mastectomy. This was a serious problem due to the axillary dissection and the removal of the axillary lymph nodes'

While working there, I received a postcard signed by President Eisenhower with a big sign: GREETINGS. I reported to the local draft Board, passed the physical examination, and informed them that I was a physician. I was told that I would enter the service as a Commissioned Medical officer, and given the rank of Captain since I had been out of Medical School more than five years. I was ordered to report to Fort Sam Houston in San Antonio, Texas in March 1955. I was proud to have the opportunity to serve in the Armed Forces of my adoptive country, and I was looking forward to crossing the Hudson River and to get to know America.

X

Mother and I made a small vacation of it. We drove to Washington D.C., and from there through Appalachia to New Orleans where we spent a couple of days. It was in New Orleans that I saw for the first and only time in my life separate seating arrangements for Negroes and Caucasians in a city autobus. Mother took a plane back to New York, and I continued to San Antonio.

At Fort Sam Houston in our barrack, we were all doctors and dentists, commissioned officers, outranking the second Lieutenant in charge of our basic training. We went through drills, infiltration courses, and firing M2 rifles. After about three weeks, a Colonel from the Surgeon General's office addressed us about our assignments. He asked us to write down three requests; he said that he could not promise us an assignment to the first request, but that he was pretty sure he could guarantee one of the three. I was interested to learn more about the United States, and I wrote down Florida, Colorado and California. In the afternoon we each had private interview with the Colonel. He looked at my requests, looked at me, and asked: "Do you want to go to Europe or to Japan?" I said: "Sir, I have three requests Florida, Colorado, California" and he said: "I am asking you again; do you want to go to Europe or to Japan?" I answered: "I am saying again Florida, Colorado, California". "O.K." he said, "you will go to Europe", and I said: "Yes, sir".

I was to report to Camp Kilmer, N.J., to be shipped to Europe. I was given five days travel time from San Antonio to the port of embarkation. Since I wanted to have a couple of free days in New York, 1 drove non-stop from San Antonio to exit 13 of the Pennsylvania Turnpike, where my car broke down. My car was a Mercury, so I had it towed to a Ford dealership just off exit 13.

The mechanic of the Chambersburg Ford Motor Company examined my Mercury, and found that the transmission had burned out He felt that it would take two to three days to get the parts and repair it. I explained to the manager that I did not have the time because I was on my way overseas. The manager gave me the option of trading in my 1950 Mercury for a new 1955 Ford and to finance the balance. The Chambersburg Ford Motor Company arranged the financing, and assured me that I could have the car shipped overseas.

I proceeded in my new automobile to New York, where I spent one day with my mother and seeing some friends, and I reported the following day to Camp Kilmer for embarkation. The sergeant at the transportation office asked me if I owned the automobile, and I told him yes, I owned it, but there was a mortgage. He informed me that I would have to have a written authorization by the mortgage holder to ship the car to Europe. I told him that I would not have a problem, and I called the Chambersburg Ford Motor Company asking them to send me such an authorization. They told me on the phone that, in spite of their verbal assurances, they would not send me a written authorization. The sergeant felt sorry for me, and he looked at me and said: "Captain, you are an officer and a gentleman, you tell me the car is yours, and I will ship it". I remembered Nonna's saying" It takes a lifetime to prove that one is honest, but only one instant that one is a liar". "Sergeant," I said, "officers and gentlemen do not lie, the car has a mortgage". "Sorry", he replied," I can not ship it, Sir". "I understand," I said.

I drove the car to the nearest Ford dealer, the Landis Ford Co. in New Brunswick, N.J., told them about my predicament, and was told that the best they could do is to take in the car, which now was a used car with only a few hundred miles on the odometer, and was worth, according to them, only the amount of the mortgage of 1834.85 dollars. I would lose my Mercury (850 dollars trade in value) and 94 dollars and 30 cents I had paid cash. I signed the car over to them. The following day I sailed on an Army transport to Europe—destination Bremerhaven.

My original orders assigned me to Paris, but upon debarkation in Bremerhaven they were changed to Bussac, outside Bordeaux. Upon reporting to the Station Hospital in Bussac, I was told by the Commanding Officer that they did not need a surgeon, and I was moved by ambulance to La Rochelle, where the COMZ (communication zone) headquarters were located. There I was assigned to the 28th General Hospital located in La Rochelle in an old building, which had been used by the French Army as a Hospital during Napoleon's times. I would remain there for the duration of my tour of duty, and those 21 months became mostly happy times.

Even ten years after the end of World War II, and after the Marshall Plan had been in existence for several years, the population in France and throughout Europe was far from prosperous, and lacked most luxuries. There were very few automobiles in circulation, and cosmetics and American cigarettes were at a premium. Gasoline was available to American officers and soldiers at the PX for ten cents a gallon, Revelon and other cosmetics, and nylon stockings were also available at the PX at low prices, and each member of the Armed Forces was allowed to purchase at the PX one carton of cigarettes a week for one dollar.

It does not take a vivid imagination to figure out that it was quite advantageous to a French family to have a friendly relationship with a member of the American Armed Forces. All Officers, single or married, with or without family, lived on the economy, and received a special monthly living allowance. There were American Schools for dependent children, and there were American civilian teachers and secretaries, called Dependent of the Army Civilians or DAC. All this made sex readily available, with material rewards on the minds of French women, and "romance" on the mind of American women.

I lived in a house on the beach in Chatellaion, a few miles south of La Rochelle. Obviously I needed transportation, and I purchased a used Hillman from a DAC who was returning to the US, but I wanted the Ford Motor Company to know how poorly one of their dealers had treated me and how they had lied to me. I wrote a letter on June 12th, 1955, to the General Manager of the Ford Motor Company in Detroit, describing in detail my poor experience and my material loss at a time when I could least afford it. I found out that the arrogance and hypocrisy of the corporate world has no limits, and that "the customer comes first" is a myth. Several weeks later I received an answer from the Ford Motor Company, signed by a secretary, stating that the company had no control over their dealers, and that there was not one thing they could do about what had happened. The letter did not express one word of regret or apology.

I have purchased many automobiles since then, but never a Ford product. I have also asked my children not to buy Ford products, and so far they have followed my request.

A few months after I had arrived at La Rochelle, my Commanding Officer, Colonel Pullen, called me to his office and said: "Captain, you are not an American citizen!" "I know", I answered. Col. Pullen continued: "You can not be a Commissioned Officer unless you are a citizen". "The Commission was given to me, I did not steal it," I said. "I know. I know," he said," what are you doing on Saturday?" "Nothing" I said. "Good" he said "be at the Officer's Club at 1100 hour, and bring a witness". I arrived at the La Rochelle Officers' Club at 11 o'clock with my friend Major Nelson. The Army had flown in from Washington D.C. a representative of the Justice Department, and I was sworn in a citizen of the United States. The date was December 3rd, 1955, and my certificate bears the number O.S. (overseas) 11100.

While I was in La Rochelle, my Mother went to Firenze for 6 months and stayed with our cousins. She also came to visit me for a few days and enjoyed her stay very much.

During the summer of 1956 the American Forces in Europe were placed on alert. In March of that year France had recognized the independence of Morocco and Tunisia. In June 1956 Colonel Nasser, unopposed, was elected President of Egypt, and on July 26th President Nasser announced the seizure of the property of the Suez Canal Company. This action had been preceded by a long controversy about the construction and the funding of the Aswan Dam. Britain and France protested this seizure but received no support from the U.S. Government. Egypt, in defiance of International Law barred Israeli vessels from entering the Suez Canal and Israel attacked Egypt. British and French troops occupied Port Said at the North end of the Suez Canal, but President Eisenhower put pressure on Great Britain, France and Israel and in December 1956 British, French, and Israeli forces withdrew from the Suez Canal. This action by President Eisenhower undermined British and French influence in the Middle East, reinforced President Nasser's influence in the Arab world, and probably contributed to the strengthening of Arab and Islamic fundamentalism in the Middle East.

At about the same time (November 4th, 1956) the Soviet forces entered Hungary and occupied Budapest in support of the "peasant worker" Government of Janos Kadar. The Hungarian Prime Minister Imre Nagy appealed to the U.N. and to the Western Powers for assistance against the Soviet invasion. Neither the U.N. nor President Eisenhower lifted one finger. The alert of the American Forces in Europe was cancelled.

During the fall of 1956 I had become Chief of Surgery of the 28th General Hospital, replacing Major Lynch. Doctor Mansfield, Professor of Neurosurgery at the University of Cincinnati, came to inspect the 28th General Hospital on behalf of the Surgeon General's office, in spite of the fact that we did not have a neurosurgical unit He spent three days with us, and enjoyed the beach at my house in Chatellaion. When I took him to the railroad station for his trip to the Army Hospital in Stuttgart, he asked me if I was going to stay in the Service, I said no, that I would return to New York and private life. He said that surgeons were a dime a dozen in New York, and that I should consider the Midwest. I said that the only people I knew were in New York, and he suggested that I might just take another year of residency in the Midwest in order to get acquainted. I said that I would not mind another year of residency, but that I would not like to start at the bottom again. His last words while he was getting on the train were: "I'll see what I can do". I thought that this conversation was strictly cocktail talk, but about six weeks later I received a letter from Doctor Mansfield thanking me for the hospitality, and saying that Akron City Hospital had lost the man slated to be Chief surgical resident starting July 1st, 1957, and that he had talked to the Chief of the Surgical Department Doctor Schlueter about me, and that if I wanted the job, it was mine.

I went to the library to learn about Akron, Ohio. It was listed as "rubber capital of the world". It can't be all bad, I thought. I applied for a license to practice by reciprocity with my license in Maine, and I obtained it by return mail. I then applied for the job at Akron City Hospital. On January 16th, 1957 I received the following letter: "Dear Captain Krahl: it gives me great pleasure to inform you that the chief of our surgical service, Dr. Schlueter, and staff have reviewed favorably your application for a fourth year senior residency in surgery. You would be very proud of the unqualified endorsements given you by Drs. Habif, Mansfield, and Rousselot. I am sure that this praise was well earned by you. When you return to the States please visit us so that you may tour the hospital and learn about our teaching program. Very truly yours, Thomas R. Kelly, M.D. Director of Medical Education.

I finished my tour of duty and returned to the United States with a small detour to Firenze and Rome. It was a very pleasant experience to see again relatives, teachers and friends wearing the uniform of a Medical Corps Officer of the United States Army. It gave me the feeling that I had achieved something in my life that only few years earlier would have been considered impossible to achieve. After a few days I returned to New York again on a military transport and, after honorable discharge, I went to work again with Doctor Habif, until it was time to go to Akron.

XI

On July 1st, 1957 I started my duties at Akron City Hospital. In September of that year I met Anne Katharine Ferbstein. It was truly "love at first site". We were married on June 14th, 1958 in her Parents' home. My Mother moved to Akron and we rented an apartment for her a few blocks from where our apartment was. On July 1st of that year I started my private practice in general and vascular surgery with an office in the Second National Building in Akron, Ohio. Our son Ned was born at Akron City Hospital on March 26th, 1959.

If in New York surgeons were a dime a dozen, there was no shortage of surgeons in Akron, and although I was making a reasonable living, I was not as busy as I wanted to be. There was also the question of "referrals". Specialists are usually not chosen by the patient, but they are introduced to the patient by the family physician, therefore the practice of a specialist depends on the "good will" of the family physicians. Although I was reasonably busy, I would have preferred to work in a part of the country where my services were needed, rather than being "indebted" to the referring physician. In the meantime I took the specialty Board examinations in surgery and passed them. The written exams were held in Cleveland, and the oral exams were held in Cincinnati.

Doctor Foderick, with whom I had worked on the House staff of Akron City Hospital, and who was Canadian by birth, had settled in Superior, Wisconsin; he was very busy and needed help. He asked me to join him as a full partner. The offer was vary attractive, but I wanted Anne, born and raised in Akron, with family and friends in Akron, to make the decision. She did while we were visiting Superior in January 1960.

XII

Life in Superior, a town of about 30.000, was quite different from the life in Akron. We bought a house from an attorney, John Davis. He introduced me to Clarence Kinney, owner of the local Bank and Trust Company, and told him that I would join Dr. Foderick, and that we had agreed on the price of the house, 21.000 dollars. Clarence asked: "How much money do you want to put up for the down payment?" "As little as possible" I answered. "How about nothing?" Clarence asked, "That will be fine", I said. "How much would you like to pay per month?" Clarence asked again "As little as possible", I answered. "O.K.", Clarence continued, "You must pay the interest which is 5½%. You can make payments on the principal whenever you want to". "This is fine," I said. "John give him the keys," Clarence said, and we shook hands. So much for business in a small town in Mid-America in those days. Hugh Fitzpatrick had been right: life was different west of the Hudson River. We moved into our new home April 1st, 1960.

When we moved to Superior, my Mother followed us. She lived first in an apartment, and later in a small house. Our daughter Kate was born in Superior on July 13th, 1961. My Mother's life was filled with joy by the arrival of Her grandchildren, and She had a good influence on their lives. The children, affectionately, called her "Nonna".

The partnership with John Foderick did not work out. We had sealed it with a handshake, and we broke it up with a handshake, and we remained good friends. We were envisioning our careers differently. Seven other local physicians and I formed a multi specialty clinic, and named it "The Superior Clinic", and I became the first President. We built a new clinic building next to a new hospital, "The Superior Memorial Hospital".

Remembering what Clarence Kinney had done for me when I first came to town, I suggested that the building mortgage of the Clinic building and the bank account of the Superior Clinic itself be placed with Kinney's Community Bank and Trust Company. Eventually we became his largest account. The practice flourished. I was the youngest member of the group, and, as a surgeon, the biggest producer. I enjoyed very much being busy, and we were all a "happy family".

The world was not quite as serene. There had been the Cuban missile crisis, and the French had been forced years before to leave South East Asia after the battle of Dien Bien Phu. The United States had become involved in Viet Nam when President Kennedy had sent "military advisers" to South Vietnam in 1962. President Kennedy had been assassinated in Dallas, Texas on November 22, 1963, and his assassin, Lee Harvey Oswald, had been killed in prison, in full view of a television audience two days later. The official enquiry never reached a completely satisfactory explanation, and an air of mystery and suspension persisted. President Johnson intensified the Vietnam war. To do so he created the "Tomkin incident" followed by a congressional resolution bearing the same name. Eventually Secretary of Defense McNamara's "memoirs" confirmed these misrepresentations, but years later. "Weapons of mass destruction" would be used by President Bush many years later as an excuse to invade Iraq. I wonder if Secretary of Defense Rumsfeld will one day write his "memoirs".

President Johnson sent thousands of troops, and bombed North Vietnam. Over 50.000 American soldiers died in Viet Nam. It was not a popular war, and it somehow changed the meaning of the term "duty". It became acceptable to be a draft dodger, and it became o.k. to go to Canada, or to take another college course to avoid the draft.

At the same time the Vietnam War changed the meaning of the term "duty", the contraceptive "pill" helped to reinterpret the term "honor". Young women had been refraining from prenuptial intercourse in the name of "honor", but mainly for fear of out of wedlock pregnancy. Now that easy contraception had become readily available, intercourse became a more frequent occurrence among young unmarried women, and "honor" became a second consideration to safety. During the days of my youth, no teenager would even think about sex with a girl from "a good family". Romance was something to dream about. As time went on, it became acceptable to live with a member of the opposite sex without being married. It became referred to as a "relationship". I would say that a partnership was a marriage without the benefit of intercourse, and that a relationship was intercourse without the benefit of marriage.

Paradoxically, just as President Johnson and his Administration were responsible for the fiasco and the sacrifices of the Vietnam War, so, and on the positive side, they became responsible for the long overdue legal abolition of segregation in the American public schools and in American society. They also were responsible for providing healthcare to American senior citizens through the creation of the Medicare program, which passed the Senate by one vote.

In 1970, 25 years after the end of World War Two, Anne and I, with 20 other surgeons and their spouses, went to Moscow, Leningrad, Stockholm and Copenhagen for a series of surgical conferences. After arrival at the Moscow airport, we were taken by bus to our hotel. The bus stopped a couple of miles outside the city limits for one minute, and we asked why. Our Russian guide told us that all traffic stopped there to commemorate the line where the Russian Army stopped the German troops in the winter of 1942. It made us realize how close the fall of Moscow had come, and perhaps a change in the outcome to the war and in the history of the world. Remember the refusal of the Serb Army to surrender causing a one-month delay in the German invasion of Russia?

Life in Moscow in those days was drab. Hospital equipment was outdated. At that time most equipment in American Hospitals was disposable, in Russia they were still reutilizing syringes, drapes, gloves and I.V. tubing. Labor was cheap and there was full employment. The techniques, however, were advanced. The stapling of lung tissue, and the use of staples for intra-abdominal anastomosis was actually started in those days in Russia. They were also experimenting with blood transfusions using blood from cadavers. Medical care, in Hospitals and for outpatients was free including medicines. Abortion was the only procedure that was not free, but it was available on demand during the first trimester of pregnancy, and for the equivalent of about ten dollars.

The doctors' income in Russia at that time was only slightly above the nurses' income and just about equal to other professions. Politicians, artists, astronauts and scientists enjoyed higher incomes, but far below the equivalent incomes in non-communist countries.

We flew from Moscow to Leningrad on a Russian aircraft. For the first and only time in my life did I witness planned "standing room" on an airplane. There were actually handles hanging from the ceiling of the airplane's cabin where passengers could hang onto, just like an autobus. And there were actually passengers riding "standing room class". Life in Leningrad seemed happier and more open than in Moscow.

In Stockholm the hospitals, equipment and techniques were up to date, and very similar to how things were done in the United States. The difference was in the economics of medicine since they operated on a socialized system. Doctors worked on a schedule and a salary. It reminded me of the way I had practiced medicine while I was in the Army. The income of the surgeons in Sweden was lower than our average incomes in private practice, and their taxes were relatively higher, but their standard of living was equal and perhaps higher than ours. Healthcare was free, their children's education was free, and their retirement income was guaranteed and close to their salaries. Should they get sick their salaries would continue. They actually did not have to save money, and could spend all their income, and they did not have to plan financially for tomorrow.

Anne and I were having dinner one evening with a Swedish surgeon and his wife and were comparing our ways of life, when the Swedish surgeon suddenly said: "your Government in the United States is spending too much money on armaments". I replied: "You may be right, but if we did not spend so much money on armaments, Sweden might have become a Russian province a long time ago". He looked at me perplexed, and the conversation turned to a different subject. I think I was right, and perhaps he did too.

In 1965 we moved to a new home, located on a cliff at the very end of Lake Superior, and surrounded by five acres of woods. Jokingly I would say that we had moved to an integrated neighborhood because from our kitchen window we could see a white birch tree and a black pine tree growing a few feet apart. During the summer, in the evenings and weekends we would enjoy boat rides from our dock in front of the house. It reminded me of my childhood in Abbazia at the North end of the Adriatic. Quite often these rides were interrupted by emergency calls. I was available and working 24 hours a day, seven days a week, and enjoying it. In the winter, the lake at our end was frozen, and we would take snowmobile rides or go cross-country skiing.

The way medicine was being practiced in the United States was slowly changing, and the personal relationship between doctor and patient that had made being a doctor very rewarding and respected, was becoming progressively more impersonal with the increased interference of third parties, and the loss of trust. As the desire for second opinions and the fear of malpractice lawsuits increased, the happy patient-doctor relationship decreased. Being a healthcare provider became less of a vocation and more of a business. And when healthcare providers started to advertise, things got even worse. Have you ever seen a fire station or a courthouse advertise? Why should hospitals advertise? People do not go to a hospital to have a good time or a vacation. The purpose of a hospital is to provide healthcare, not to attract customers who do not need the service. They should not try to enhance their image at the expense of another institution, nor damage the reputation of another hospital. Hospitals should cooperate to better serve the public, and not try to outmaneuver the competition. It should not be handled as a business, but as a service. There is no need for competition. There should be cooperation.

Competition in medicine increases the cost to the consumer. Duplication of equipment that is not fully utilized, increases the cost, does not lower it. The cost of healthcare has been rising dramatically: from about 6% of GNP forty years ago, to about 16% of GNP.

The major reasons for this dramatic increase are:

1.   New and expensive technology

2.   Competition among providers with large advertising and administrative costs

3.   Defensive medicine

4.   Lack of foreign competition

5.   Demand on the part of the consumer of "the best possible" rather than "adequate" healthcare, with the implied threat of malpractice lawsuits.

Society cannot afford the best possible care for everybody, but should supply adequate care to everybody. If one looks at LIFE objectively, one will find that everything is actually "rationed" according to one's emotional, physical and financial situation. Why should one presume to have the "right" to unlimited healthcare? When it comes to National Security, decisions have to made by the Department of Defense on how to divide the allocated resources and get an adequate supply of tanks, ships and airplanes within a budget, though each Service would probably like to have more. Adjustments are made when dictated by experience. The same principle should be applied to healthcare, and changes eventually made when advisable. Society should determine what is "adequate care" within an established and affordable budget. In the final analysis the consumer is paying for the healthcare, regardless of what hat the consumer is wearing (direct payer, payer of the insurance premiums, or taxpayer).

Members of the Superior Clinic continued to work in harmony year after year. The older members were eventually replaced with new members, and new members were also added as the clinic grew. As President of the Clinic, I would interview the new prospective Doctors, and, as years went by, I would hear less and less questions like" what kind of work can I expect to be doing?" and more and more questions like "how much money can I make and how much time off can I expect to get?". I was the last of the founding members to retire on April 30th, 1984.

My decision to retire, perhaps earlier than I had originally planned, was probably also based on the above stated ways the practice of medicine had been changing. A few years after I had retired, the Superior Clinic was absorbed by the much larger Duluth Clinic. The members probably became able to work less and make more money.

Ned and Kate had grown up very well, going to public schools and seeming to enjoy the atmosphere of the Upper Midwest based on fiscal conservatism and social liberalism. They had graduated from College with Master degrees, were employed, and were living on their own. My Mother had died in Superior in February 1984, and Anne and I had taken Her ashes to Fiume (now Rjieka, Yugoslavia) to be buried next to my Father.

Anne and I liked very much the life in Superior, and we had made many good friends over the years, but the winters were very long, and we decided that, after retirement, we would move to a more favorable climate, and chose Savannah, Georgia as our new residence. We settled in our new home in Savannah in March 1985.

XIII

Had Emperor Constantine not have seen a burning cross while he was having a nightmare, and had he not subsequently established toleration of Christianity by signing with Licinius the edict of Milan in 313, paganism might have survived a few more centuries, and society today might have been a secular democracy. It took 400 years for Christianity to undermine the Roman Empire. It may take I don't know how many years for Islam to destroy Western Civilization, unless we can succeed in making them change their fundamentalist ways.

Fundamentalism of all denominations is intolerant and destructive, and has caused pain and tragedies throughout history, and continues to do it today. The most fundamentalist and cruel period of the Catholic Church occurred in the 14th and 15th centuries, when the Inquisition was rampant. The "infidels" had the option of converting or being expelled or killed. Most of them were executed by hanging or burned at the stake.

Mohamed was born about six centuries after Jesus Christ, and Islam started about six centuries after Christianity. Islam has reached the peak of fundamentalism in the 20th and 21st centuries, six centuries after the Inquisition. History does seem to repeat itself. During the Inquisition "infidels" could be killed only one at a time; today's weapons of mass destruction make fundamentalist Islam much more dangerous. The fundamentalism of the Catholic Church was curbed internally, by men like Hus, Luther, and Calvin. Fundamentalists can be killed from the outside, but fundamentalism can only be curbed and eliminated from the inside. We can only hope that history will again repeat itself, and that Islam can produce some enlightened Mullahs who will bring about an Islamic Reformation.

It is really too bad, however, and quite tragic that fundamentalism of one denomination was followed in history by fundamentalism of another denomination. Humanity would have gained a great deal, in my opinion, had fundamentalism been followed sometime in history by liberal secularism.

I have often wondered how history would have unfolded had President Carter chosen to give the Ayatollah Khomeini an ultimatum when American hostages were taken in November 1979. Had President Carter, instead of negotiating with the fanatics of the Iranian Government, and eventually sending a few helicopters to try and rescue the hostages, told the Iranian Government that they had x number of hours to release all the hostages unharmed, or, had they failed to do so, that Teheran would have been turned into another Hiroshima, I do not know how the Iranian Government would have reacted. I believe, however, that either way, the Islamic fanatics would have gotten a message that could have avoided the many subsequent problems that region and those fanatics have caused during the past 25 years. I also believe that President Carter would have won reelection by a wide margin. Of course we will never know, because in life there is no rehearsal.

In lay life a dictatorship is the equivalent of fundamentalism in religion. Remember the banners across all the streets in Italy during my childhood? "Il Duce ha sempre ragione", the Duce is always right. Dictators have all the answers, they are never wrong. They get their authority from their power. Religious fundamentalists claim their authority as given to them by God! And they don't have to prove anything.

Just as there are two sides to every coin, there are at least two points of view on every issue. Most times one's freedom fighter is someone else's terrorist, and someone's terrorist is someone else's freedom fighter. It is however always naive to believe that "freedom fighters" want independence for their people: they really want power for themselves.

By the same token it is very helpful to represent a very powerful country when one is defying international Law. Milosevic, certainly no saint, was indicted for crimes against Humanity, but President Johnson and Secretary MacNamara were never indicted for their Vietnam adventure. We bombed Serbia for trying to prevent the breakup of Yugoslavia, but we consider President Lincoln a great man for preventing the breakup of the Union, and sending General Sherman on his march to the sea, doing essentially to the Southern States what Milosevic tried to do to the breakaway provinces of Yugoslavia, The "Truth" is usually relative to a point of view, and history is and has always been written by the victor.

We should try and be more consistent in our judgments, after having reflected carefully about the issues. If we all were able to behave and act this way, the world we live in would be a much better place, and we would not have to dream about Heaven, it would be right here with us on Earth.

Traveling through Tuscany and Umbria one becomes very aware of the hilltop towns and the castles in the center of those towns. These castles remind us of the political structure and the social life of the late Middle Ages and the early Renaissance, when feudal regimes were supreme. The Princes and the Dukes were the arbiters of the lives of their subjects. They were supported by their courtiers, and they made sure that the courtiers were compensated for doing so. The enlighten-ment and the French Revolution changed matters for a while, but the same cus-toms have resurfaced, and very little has really changed today except for the names. The Princes and the Dukes have become the CEO's, and the courtiers have become the members of the Board of Directors. The peasants are still pow-erless peasants, only now they are called workers and stockholders. A CEO may dismiss thousands of workers, cut the stockholders' dividend, and at the same time pay himself a bonus for the great job he is doing, and of course also throw some crumbs to the Board of Directors. The one big difference is that in the old days if a Prince or a Duke lost a battle, they would pay with their lives, today the losing CEO gets a golden parachute. The Enron collapse, where corporate greed and concomitant Board and accounting complicity created a situation in which the workers and the stockholders lost everything is a scandalous example of such a conduct. It is always a tragic situation, amoral and pernicious, when the CEO lets thousands of workers go in order to "save costs", when the stockholders' dividend is cut for the same reason, and when, at the same time, the CEO, other top man-agers, and members of the Board get a large bonus for "superb leadership".

The decrease in the income tax rate for the very wealthy enacted during the Reagan Administration, and the further tax cuts during the G.W. Bush Adminis-tration caused not only growing deficits in the Federal Budget, but also an increase in the "greed factor", and a much wider spread between the very rich on one side, and the middle class and the poor on the other. The "middle class" has always been the backbone of the American society. If this trend is not reversed, and hopefully it will be, it may eventually cause severe social unrests.

The ills of unbridled capitalism are just as bad as the ills of other economic systems. Business should always be conducted in an open and honest way, regard-less of economic system, and Governments at all levels should make sure that all interests are balanced and safeguarded. It has always amused me that the battle cry of most "conservative" politicians and businessmen of the second half of the 20th century has been: "Smaller Government", and "keep the Government out", forgetting that most of them owed their education and therefore their success to the G.I. Bill, one of the most expensive, greatest, and certainly most successful Government programs. What might have become of them without this program? How quickly people forget!

Today people want to know more and more about technology, they want real-ity, and they want it now.

When a group of high school teenagers was asked: "what do you want to become when you grow up?", the most common answer was: "famous".

Romance used to be cherished in the dark. Now sex is paraded in full bright light, and tenderness has been replaced by Viagra. Also today the crowning glory for a community is not the acquiring of a new industry or a new University, but the acquiring of a foot-ball franchise or a baseball franchise; foot-ball and baseball used to be the American pastimes; they are becoming the main industries.

We are not geared to producing goods any longer, we are geared to producing entertainment. Has anyone ever thought of the meaning of the term "decadence"?

1980 became a year with history shaping events: the continued presence of Soviet troops in Afghanistan, described by President Carter as the "greatest threat to peace since World War Two" would eventually translate into U.S. support for Afghan fighters, and the consolidation of the Taliban. The death of President Tito of Yugoslavia, replaced by a collective Presidency, would eventually lead to the breakup of the country. Occupation by strikers of the Lenin shipyard in Gdansk, and the formation of independent trade unions in Poland would mark the first crack in the Soviet block in Eastern Europe. The invasion of Iran by Iraq in an attempt to gain control of the Shatt-al Arab waterway would bring U.S. support to Saddam Hussein. Very few people would have predicted then the long-range dramatic consequences of all these events.

The following year the U.S. Center for Disease Control recognized Aids (Acquired Immune Deficiency Syndrome) thought to be caused by the HIV virus. The first cases were reported in homosexual males, and I believe that, because of this reason, and in order to be "politically correct" the privacy rule was applied. All other contagious diseases, from measles to syphilis, have to be reported to health authorities, and an epidemiological investigation is carried out, involving all "contacts". In the case of AIDS it was decided that the privacy rule should apply. I blame the American Medical Association as much as I blame the Government for playing along in this political game instead of insisting AIDS be subjected to the same rules as other communicable diseases. There was no known treatment for AIDS then, and there is still no effective treatment. When there was no effective treatment against leprosy, society protected itself by isolating lepers; this time not only were HIV positive people not isolated, their anonymity was protected by the "privacy act" and they were allowed to knowingly or unknowingly transmit the deadly virus in geometric progression.

A few years later, in October 1993, I brought this matter to the attention of Kristine M. Gebbie, RN, MN, National AIDS policy coordinator in President Clinton's Administration, and her position was that: "it would be more advisable to improve the nature of the prevention messages that we are delivering to population at risk rather than trying to limit the civil liberties of those infected".

I still believe that when your actions spread a deadly disease, you lose "the civil liberties" that allow you to spread the disease and thereby kill other people. I am convinced that the disease would have been much better controlled had the rules governing other infectious diseases been followed.

The catastrophic spread of this disease in Africa only confirms, I believe, my point of view.

1989 was a year of great change. In March Boris Yeltsin was elected in Moscow by a very large margin, running against communist party officials. In April Lech Walesa and the Polish Government signed an agreement for political and economic reforms. In June President Gorbachev and Chancellor Kohl of West Germany signed an agreement affirming the right of European States to determine their own political system. In October a new Hungarian Republic was declared allowing multi party democracy. In November the Berlin wall started to come down. A few years later Anne and I were in Berlin and had a German tour guide doing nothing except denouncing the Russians for what they had done in East Berlin. After a while I became tired of his condemnations, and I said: "You know, had you not gone to Moscow, the Russians would not have come here, so blame Hitler or shut up".

In December 1989 President Ceaucescu of Rumenia was executed by the army, and Vaclav Havel was elected Czekoslovakia's first non-communist President in 41 years.

During the 1990's while Congress was ruminating about "term limits", a thought occurred to me that would, in my opinion, take care of term limits and also make true the term "to serve the public". Today most politicians make a career out of politics, and use the term" to serve the public" as an excuse for their self-interest.

The Constitution states that a candidate must be at least 35 years old to run for the Presidency, and at least 30 years old to run for the Senate, therefore age has already been established as a valid requirement for Federal Office. Two hundred years ago 30 and 35 years of age represented upper middle age, comparable to 55 or 60 years today.

I would like to see the Constitution amended so as to state that a candidate must be at least 60 years of age to run for Federal Office (Congress, the Senate, and the Presidency). This would take care in most cases of "term limits", and would give credence to the words "to serve the public". Candidates would run for Federal Office not to make a career if it, but after they had a career in the private sector, had been successful and had gained useful life experiences, and were now truly ready to "serve the public". I shared these thoughts with my two Georgia Senators, but my letters remained unanswered.

Throughout his 1992 Presidential campaign Bill Clinton vowed to make healthcare reform a cornerstone of his Presidency, and shortly after his inauguration he created a taskforce putting his wife Hillary in charge of the taskforce.

On February 23,1993 I wrote her the following letter:

"I am taking the liberty of writing to you in the hope that the points I will raise may be of some help to you in the difficult job you have undertaken. We all know that the present system is not fair and is not cost effective. The only fair, effective and affordable system is one providing basic healthcare to all citizens under a prepaid comprehensive coverage offered by Health Care Maintenance Organizations (call it managed care, if you wish). For this system to succeed financially, two basic changes have to be introduced and accepted by the public: the malpractice mania has to be eliminated, and the public has to understand the concept of adequate care vs. unlimited care. Malpractice, Defensive medicine is wasteful, and high awards do not punish the culprit but increase the cost of healthcare for everybody through higher insurance premiums. The Wisconsin panel system should be adopted nationally, and improved upon after more experience is gained. Under this system, all cases should be reviewed by a panel composed by a lawyer (chair) two physicians and two people from the jury list. The findings of the panel should be admissible as evidence if either the plaintiff or the defendant are not satisfied with the decision of the panel and decide to go to court. Damages should be compensated along the guidelines set by workmen's compensation, and doctors who show a pattern of negligence should be penalized by suspending or revoking their license. Adequate care. Prepaid comprehensive coverage can only work, and be fair to both the provider and the consumer, if the services to be provided are properly outlined. The Oregon Plan should be used as a model and improved after it has been tried. Providing all the services people would like to have would promptly bankrupt the system. Cost effectiveness must be considered. The public must understand that, since a finite amount of money is available, choices have to be made. For example, one might have to choose between providing a liver transplant to a deathly sick child or use the same money to provide one million glasses of milk to one million undernourished but otherwise healthy children. Today's system of reimbursement to hospitals, based on cost plus concept is rewarding the inefficient and the greedy. Hospitals should not need a marketing director any more than a courthouse or a fire station need a marketing director. Hospitals should cooperate with each other, and not compete with each other at the expense of the consumer, duplicating expensive equipment and services that are not fully utilized. One can hardly justify the salary of a hospital administrator being higher than the salary of the President of the United States; still hospitals have been increasing their administrative costs at the expense of the cost of patient care and education. Providers' fees are too high, and continue to rise. Management and labor in American industry combined years ago to increase production costs to a point where foreign made products put them out of business. There is no foreign competition in health care, and the providers take advantage of it and continue to increase their fees, and the consumer has no recourse but to pay them. Surgical and obstetrical fees are much too high. The February 1993 issue of Medical Economics for Surgeons shows that 74% have a first year gross earnings in excess of 150.000 dollars. Radiologists and anesthesiologists earn hundreds of thousands of dollars a year working three days a week. Managed care can change this. One requirement to make the system work is that the providers must be enrolled full time in this system. If they are allowed to work "part time" in both systems, they would eventually sabotage the managed care system because their livelihood would not depend on it The providers who do not wish to join the managed care groups should be free to do so but they would have to rely entirely on wealthy patients who are paying for their care out of their own pocket or through some special insurance covering fee for service. A Federal licensing system, replacing State licensing, would be desirable. It would standardize performance throughout the system and would make services readily available throughout the country. For the purpose of staffing underserved areas the same incentive could be used as the Military Academies use when they provide free education for a payback of an equal number of years in the Armed Forces. Federally sponsored full scholarships in medical education could be offered using a payback of an equal number of years in an underserved area. A temporary license could be issued for that purpose, to be replaced by a regular license only after that particular obligation has been completed. This method would avoid the abuse of college loans that are never repaid. These scholarships and licensing methods could apply to doctors as well as nurses, technicians, etc. All this should be part of a long-range plan. To improve the immediate need of cost controls, a more stringent cap on reimbursement should be introduced, forcing providers who sign up for the Medicare and Medicaid programs to accept the reimbursement as payment in full. As to paying for the long-range program, I believe that the easiest and the fairest way to do it, is to finance the entire program through a VAT. Once the cost is estimated, and Government contributions (Medicare Medicaid) from the Federal Government as well as State and local Governments are deducted from the total estimated cost, the percentage of the VAT necessary to cover the balance is calculated. To compensate the consumer for the added cost of the VAT, employers who will save the cost of healthcare coverage, should increase the salary of each employee by the amount of the cost of their previous health coverage. The Government will benefit from taxes on the increased income. The

Federal Government would further save VA and military dependents health costs, now covered by the national plan. VA facilities could become the nucleus for long-term care. To minimize abuses in utilization, a token payment should be required for each service. Perhaps as little as one dollar for indigent people and five dollars for the average person. Your job is a tough one. I wish you well".

Not having heard from her or her staff, I sent another letter on September 3, 1994. Here it is: "On February 23, 1993 I wrote you a letter as Chair of the Task Force on Health Care Reform which was never acknowledged by you or by your staff. At this point the needed health care reform seems to be in limbo. Pointing to the insurance companies as the main villains in the health care crisis has not convinced either Congress or the public because we all know that the insurance companies are only the intermediaries between consumers and providers and are not directly responsible for the spiraling cost of health care. Every time the providers raise their fees or consumers ask for more services, rates charged to the consumer go up. The efficiency with which insurance companies handle the process does make a difference, but it is minimal. The big difference comes from the appetite of the consumer on one side and the greed of the provider on the other. I am enclosing copy of my letter of 2.23.93 in which I tried to bring to your attention what I think are the causes for the spiraling costs, suggesting at the same time some ideas on how to reverse this tread. I will now try to further clarify my thoughts. Free market forces do not work in the American health care industry because: a) there is no foreign competition b) competition in medicine increases the cost of doing business (see my article in A.M.A. News3.1.1985) c) it is a licensed profession allowing the members of the club to mistake a license to practice for a license to overcharge. Without foreign competition, American industries would not have downsized, but they would have continued to raise prices to the consumer. The way hospitals are reimbursed, there is no incentive to economize and inefficiency and greed are rewarded. The Boston Globe of August 23, 1994 published the salaries of the administrators of 6 hospitals in Boston. They range from 428,392 to 664,712 dollars per annum. How do these salaries compare with the salaries of the C.O.s of Bethesda Naval Hospital and Walter Reed Medical Center? Since the free market rules do not apply to the health care system as it is practiced today in the U.S., one has to shift to a system that will define the services to be rendered and the fees providers will receive for them. Government does not provide a chauffeured limousine for every citizen, but it does provide or should provide public transportation that is affordable. For the same reason Government should offer adequate basic health coverage to all citizens at an affordable price. For those people who want a chauffeured limousine and want more than the basic coverage, this should be available at their own expense, and should be supplied by providers who choose not to participate in the National Health program financed through a VAT and administered by one payer. Cost can only be controlled by clearly defining services consumers can expect to receive (Oregon plan) and the compensation for the providers. Does this mean rationing? In a sense yes, but so is everything else in life in accordance with the resources at one's disposal. Services not included in the basic plan will continue to be available at one's own expense or through specific separate insurance programs. Would such a system work? Of course it would. It works in the Armed Forces and in most large civilian clinics where most providers are on salary. Would it interfere with choice of physician? In some cases it would, if one particular physician would not sign up for the National Health System. In that case the patient would always have the option to see that physician and pay for the service directly. Would this system interfere with scientific progress? Probably not, since most discoveries are made in laboratories by people who are on salaries. Would it lower the quality of health care? On the contrary, I believe it would improve the quality of health care because the professional atmosphere of a multispecialty group is conducive to collective excellence. See Mayo Clinic, Cleveland Clinic, Ochsner Clinic standards and reputations vs. individual practices. Would it mean a new tax? The VAT would be a national sales tax replacing the cost of the premiums of present health care insurance. Food in grocery stores should be excluded, but not restaurants. People with more money who make more purchases would pay more, which is fair, but everybody would pay something. Even Harry and Louise[1] could understand this approach. I hope you and your staff will give these suggestions due consideration, and share your reaction with me". I never heard from Mrs. Clinton or her staff, and we all know what happened to the healthcare reform plan.

When I was approaching my 70th birthday, I wanted to do something meaningful. It is a time in life when one tends to take inventory of one's own accomplishments and failures and of one's life in relation to society. In so doing one cannot help but look at the way society has evolved as we have grown and gone through our own life span, which usually spans three generations. I came to realize that my way of thinking, my values and my way of life were much closer to my Grandparents way of life than that of the young people at the end of the 20th

1.   TV characters who criticized health care reform.

century. What better place to reflect on these matters than the crossroad where it all began for our culture, the soil on which Prophets and Philosophers walked and created the foundations for what we consider the moral and ethical codes of our daily lives and the foundation of the political system by which we govern ourselves,

I had lived in Florence and Rome where the Renaissance and the art of governing had flourished, so for my 70th birthday I wanted to visit Israel and Greece, where the moral values of the Western World were born. Anne and I took our first Elderhostel and spent a month there. On the 22nd of April 1994 I stood near Rivavim in the Negev Desert, and I was overwhelmed by the silence and the majesty of that desert, It was not a "religious" experience, but a deep "human" experience To realize that those surroundings had inspired human beings thousands of years ago to create a spiritual single entity that would idealize their aspirations.

And now that same region had become the site of hate, violence, and destruction.

The former British mandate, Palestine had been partitioned by a U.N. resolution on November 29th, 1947 into a Jewish portion and an Arab portion. The Jews accepted the partition and the Arabs rejected it. On May 14th 1948, as the British mandate in Palestine ended, the Jewish National Council and the General Zionist Council proclaimed the establishment of the State of Israel, which was recognized by the United States and the U.S.S.R. The armies of Egypt, Jordan, Syria and Lebanon attacked the new State of Israel to destroy it, but were defeated.

Israel, a Democracy, prospered and developed bringing economic and social opportunities to its people, Jews, Christians, and Moslems. The surrounding Arab States continued to keep their people under the domination of the ruling dictators and Monarchs. Israel absorbed 800.000 Jews who were expelled by the surroundings Arab countries having left behind wealth and properties they and their ancestors had accumulated, having lived there for centuries. The Arab Nations refused to accept and absorb the 650,000 Moslems that they had urged to leave Israel, and placed them instead in "refugee camps" where they have been living for decades in a squalid environment, supported by donations from the U.S. and Europe. Acts of terror have followed acts of terror to the point where Arab terrorists assassinated eleven Israeli athletes during the Munich Olympic games in 1972. Five terrorists were also killed, but the rest were allowed to leave Germany and were given asylum in Arab countries. These countries are members of the U.N., but were not rebuffed for harboring murderers. The Arab Moslems also use suicide bombers to terrorize the civilian population of Israel. They promise a number of beautiful "virgins" in Heaven to the "martyrs", and Hezbollah, an organization supported by Iran and Syria pays 25.000 dollars to the family of each dead bomber. There have been two "intifadas" against the civilian population in Israel, one after the Oslo accords were broken by the PLO, and the other after Arafat rejected a generous peace offer by the Israeli Government mediated by President Clinton, Hopefully now, after Arafat's death, the newly elected Palestinian leadership will see the light, put an end to terrorism, and start to negotiate in good faith.

A few days after we left the desert we were in the downtown of Athens, and our guide stopped on the side of the road, pointed to a hole in the wall and said: "This is the cave where Socrates died." I had tears in my eyes.

XIV

In January 1992 Slovenia and Croatia were recognized by the European Council as Independent States. Both new countries went from a communist style Government to a capitalistic type economy.

All my properties, my home and rental properties, had been "communized" and expropriated in 1945 following the annexation of Fiume to Tito's Yugoslavia. During my trip to Fiume in 1990 I had seen that my former properties were well preserved and occupied. Of course I had never received any rent. In 1996 I contacted the Croat Embassy in Washington to enquire about the status of these properties, now that the Croat Government professed to be running a free market economy. I was informed by the Embassy that, according to the new Laws, only requests for compensation made by Croat citizens would be considered. For all practical purposes this "new Law" was just another clever trick by the Croat Government to legalize stealing since in fact none of the properties expropriated in Fiume by Tito's Yugoslav Government after World War Two were owned by Croat citizens. The inhabitants of Fiume in 1945 were Italian citizens. And this thieving Croat Government had also become a member of the U.N.

I have had the same experience regarding my properties in Hungary. My father's parents owned among other things about 6000 acres of vineyards that I inherited. These vineyards were confiscated first by Hungarian Nazis and later by the Hungarian communist Government. On November 22, 1996 I wrote the following letter to the Hungarian Embassy in Washington: "I am writing to you for information concerning property in Hungary that was seized during WW II by the Nazis and after the war by the Communist Government. 1 wonder if the present Hungarian Government is considering compensating the original rightful owners for that property, and what modalities I would have to follow to submit a claim. I would appreciate any information you might be able to give me on this subject, and I thank you for your interest in this matter".

On November 27, 1996 I received the following answer:

"With reference to your letter requesting information on compensation, please be advised of the following: Compensation for loss of property had taken place beginning with 1991. Under that program claims could be made for compensation for property lost to unjust state action since 1939. For the submission of claims two deadlines were established: for loss of property due to state action following 1949, the deadline was December 16, 1991, for loss of property between 1939 and 1949 the deadline was October 8, 1992. Due to the fact that there had been a large number of people entitled to compensation who had failed to submit their claim in time, the deadline to submit claims was reopen, and claims were again accepted between February 15 and March 16, 1994, with the final decision of Parliament that it will not be reopened in the future. For the reason above, no claims for compensation for loss of property can be submitted now or in the future".

On August 28, 1997 I wrote the following letter to Secretary Albright: "You have supported the admission of Hungary to NATO stating that the present Government was "democratic" and committed to market economy. My father's family (all His brothers, sisters, nieces and nephews) were wiped out by the Hungarian pro Nazi regime during the war. They were landowners. Their properties and my properties were confiscated. The communist regime that followed continued the same thieving policy. I enclose copy of a letter I wrote on November 21, 1996 to the Hungarian Embassy in Washington. On November 27, 1996 the Embassy replied. Copy of that letter is also enclosed. From this letter one can see that the Government is not interested in fairness, justice, reparation for past crimes nor the right to private property. It points instead to bureaucratic time frames to condone murder and thievery. Unless I can be shown a different picture, I shall urge my two Senators to vote against the admission of Hungary into NATO".

I never heard from Secretary Albright. I wrote in detail to my two Senators, Max Cleland and Paul Coverdell, asking them to vote against the admission of Hungary into NATO; they both voted in favor of it.

On August 28th, 2003 I wrote again the following letter to the Hungarian Embassy: "This is a follow up to my letter of November 22, 1996 and your reply of November 27, 1996. Under the auspices of the Hungarian Government during World War Two, my Father's brothers and sisters were murdered and our vineyards confiscated. The brothers had served with distinction as commissioned officers in the Hungarian army during World War One and were all wounded and decorated. The vineyards were in our family for over 150 years. Murder and associated robbery do not enjoy a statute of limitation in a free democratic society. Your statement that requests for just compensation will not be considered again, seems a little arbitrary and quite arrogant. You can not bring back the life of people your fascist government murdered, but you certainly can and should restore to the rightful owners the properties you have stolen, or pay a fair monetary compensation for those properties. Your Government has to assume the responsibility and the obligation to right the wrongs committed by previous governments".

On September 15, 2003 I received the following answer:

"Referring to your kind letter of August 28, 2003 directed to the consular section of the Embassy of the Republic of Hungary, this way I would like to reflect on the points mentioned in it. With the utmost of due respect, I have carefully studied the content of your enquiry and the whole Hungarian legislation on the subject of recompensation. There is no doubt whatsoever that the very sad facts enumerated in your letter have been integral part of our tragic past history. At the same time I am to admit you that the corresponding Hungarian statutes adopted by the Parliament have not opened lately further possibility to newly present applications for compensation beyond the originally established deadlines. I am so sorry for not being able to provide you the notice of what you may have expected so much felt on the basis of your letter".

On August 28th, 2003 I wrote the following letter to Secretary Powell: "I am enclosing copy of correspondence between myself and the Hungarian Embassy in Washington. The subject is self-explanatory. I am also enclosing copy of a letter I sent to former Secretary Madelaine Albright on this subject. I never heard from the Secretary. I would appreciate your comments and advice on this matter".

I never heard from Secretary Powell either.

My Grandmother used to say "can non magna can" (a dog will not eat another dog), and I do not think that I am overly cynical when I say that politicians today, if they listen at all, listen only to very large contributors.

XV

Anne and I took Ned, Kate, her husband Thom and their daughters Emma and Nina to Firenze for the Millennium. We stayed in a beautiful apartment in Palazzo Antellesi in Piazza Santa Croce. Professor Valdoni and Professor Gentile had died, but I was very happy to be able to have Countess Lucia, Professor Gentile's widow over for lunch, and to introduce my family to her. We enjoyed very much our stay, and I almost felt that LIFE had come full circle.

I have lived a long, mainly happy and fairly successful life. I have often wondered what my life might have been had Hitler not been born, or had the League of Nations enforced the Treaty of Versailles and not allowed Germany to rearm and start World War Two.

This, however, did not happen. Hitler was born, and the Western Powers through Chamberlain's lips proclaimed "peace in our time". Germany to the Western Powers represented a barrier against the Soviet Union, and the capitalistic Western Democracies always favored a capitalistic Nazi or fascist dictatorship over a communist dictatorship. The Franco regime in Spain, and many regimes in South America have born out this statement.

The enemies have changed. We are not dealing with enemy Nations, but with terrorist groups, inflamed by irrational fundamentalist beliefs and supported more or less secretly by Governments that are not strong enough to fight us openly, but that enjoy seeing us being terrorized, and hoping that terrorist attacks alone will destroy us and our way of life. Now, more than half a century after the end of World War Two, we look at the world, and what do we see? Mainly that we have not learned very much from the past, and a good example is the United Nations, which is as inept and corrupt as the League of Nations was before World War Two. This is perhaps the reason why religiuos faith is still very popular, since people hope to find in "Heaven" what they have not been able to achieve on Earth.

I wish we all had the serenity to accept the things we cannot change, the courage to try to change the things we can change, and the wisdom to know the difference. It is so much easier to let "God" take care of things rather than to assume "personal responsibility"; therefore it is still true today, as it has always been, that for bad things to happen, all it takes is for good people to do nothing. It is really up to each of us to do our very best to guard and promote the liberty and freedom that make LIFE worth living.

978-0-595-35970-7
0-595-35970-1

Printed in the United States
39525LVS00006B/514-522